KATIE SUE

Heading West

KATIE SUE
Heading West

ELEANOR CLARK

HONOR NET
THE HONOR NETWORK

O MY GRANDCHILDREN AND GREAT grandchildren. May you recognize, love, and appreciate your rich Christian heritage and the privilege of living in America, which was founded on the trust and hope we have in Jesus. May you continue the legacy.

Contents

O MY LORD AND SAVIOR, JESUS CHRIST, who has blessed me with the greatest family, life, and country. May every word bring honor and glory to Your name.

To my publisher, Jake Jones, who recognized the potential of my stories and my heart's desire to bless and encourage young readers to value their American and Christian heritage.

To my writer, Janice Thompson, who understood my love of history and breathed life into my stories with the skill of her pen.

To Annabelle Meyers who helped develop the character lessons.

Trust in the LORD *with all thine heart; and lean not unto thine own understanding. In all thy ways acknowledge him, and he shall direct thy paths.*

—Proverbs 3:5-6

"It's just so hard. I don't want to leave my best friend and my school… It's not fair!"

CHANGES IN THE AIR

CHELSEA MARIE, COME AND JOIN THE family around the campfire!" Nine-year-old Chelsea Marie glanced over as she heard her grandmother's happy voice. The youngster pushed the tiny wire-rimmed glasses up on her nose and called out, "Coming, Grand Doll."

She rose from the ground where she had been writing in the dirt with a tiny stick. To be honest, she didn't really feel like joining the others as they roasted marshmallows and sang songs around the campfire. They all seemed to be having such a happy time at the family reunion, just like every year when they met at Fort Parker, Texas, but not Chelsea Marie. She didn't know if she would ever be happy again. Not since hearing the news.

"I don't want to move!" She had written the words in the dirt, but now smeared them over with her foot, hoping no one would see. She didn't want others in the family to know how she felt, but every time she thought about moving away to Indiana, her heart nearly broke in two. How could she leave her best friend, Lindsey? How could she move away from her school and her house? The very idea made her so sad, she wanted to cry.

"We're singing one of your favorites, honey!" Chelsea Marie's grandmother called out. "Come and sing along!"

She finally walked over to the campfire and joined the rest of the family. Everyone sang at the top of their lungs—her grandmother, mother and father, her brothers, Jacob and Jared, and all of her many cousins.

"*Oh, Susanna, oh don't you cry for me!*" her grandmother, Grand Doll, sang out louder than the rest. She reached to take Chelsea Marie by the hand to do a little dance, and Chelsea Marie joined in, trying to smile. If anyone could make her feel better, Grand Doll could. Why, she could turn nearly every frown upside down in no time at all—even on a day like today, when Chelsea Marie was sad.

After they finished the song, several of the girls decided to go swimming in the lake. Some of the boys argued that they should play hide-and-seek in the old fort, but in the end, the girls won out.

"Come swimming with us!" Chelsea Marie's cousin, Rachel Ann, called.

"Not this time." Chelsea Marie shook her head and turned the other way. "Go on without me."

With a shrug, Rachel Ann headed off to join the others.

Chelsea Marie was usually the first to do outdoorsy things—like swimming, hiking, riding horses, and such. She loved to swim in the lake, especially, but today she just didn't feel like it. Instead, as her aunts, uncles, and all of the children ran off to change into their swimsuits, she sat quietly at the fire with her parents and grandmother. After a few minutes, her grandmother slipped an arm over her shoulder.

"Is everything okay, honey?" she asked.

Chelsea Marie shrugged. She didn't want to be dishonest, but didn't know if she should tell her grandmother what was really bothering her, either.

"Are you missing Poppie?" her grandmother whispered in her ear.

She nodded. Yes, she did miss having her grandfather at the family reunion. Why, things just hadn't been the same since he moved to the nursing home. But she was sad for other reasons too.

Chelsea Marie's father stood and reached for a pole. "I've been thinking about going fishing," he said. "How about coming with me?"

She shrugged. "I don't really feel like fishing, Dad, but maybe tomorrow?"

"Well, then, how about helping me make some home-made ice cream?" her mother suggested. "I'm making your favorite—vanilla with chocolate chips."

"I don't know…" She gave another shrug. Nothing sounded like much fun today, nothing at all. Even if she pretended, she couldn't make this problem go away. She didn't want to move to Indiana. Not now, not ever.

Grand Doll stood and brushed the dirt from her pants. "Would you like to go for a walk with me while the others are swimming?" Grand Doll extended her hand in Chelsea Marie's direction. "There are some wonderful walking trails here, and I know we could have a great adventure together. Would you like that?"

Finally—something that sounded like fun. Chelsea Marie nodded and stood to join her grandmother as she said, "If it's all right with my mom."

"Fine with me," her mother called out. "Just come back plenty hungry! We're roasting hot dogs on the campfire this evening and eating ice cream afterwards."

"Mmm."

"Then we'll all play games together," her mother added. "I know you love games."

"Yes, ma'am." Chelsea Marie tagged along behind Grand Doll, happy to be leaving the crowd of people. For years, she and the other children had run and played together at their family reunions, but taking a long, slow walk with her grandmother sounded like more fun right now.

As they came upon the entrance of the trail, her grandmother stopped to look at an old wagon wheel. "Well, look at that!" she said with a smile on her face. "I know a wonderful story about a wagon wheel. Maybe I'll tell it to you as we walk along."

"I'd like that." To be honest, Grand Doll could do all the talking today. Chelsea Marie just felt like being quiet and a little sad.

As they wound their way into the forest brush, Chelsea Marie took hold of her grandmother's hand. She tried not to cry, but the tears seemed to come anyway.

"What's wrong with my girl?" Grand Doll asked. "What has you so sad?"

"I…I don't want to m…move." She bowed her head and let the tears flow.

Grand Doll wrapped her in her arms. "Oh, honey, I know it's hard to trust God with the changes you're going through. But God is trustworthy, no matter what. I can tell you that firsthand, because of all of the changes I've been through in my own life!"

"It's just so hard. I don't want to leave my best friend and my school… It's not fair!"

Grand Doll ran her fingers through Chelsea Marie's hair. "Life can be very hard. And you're right—sometimes things happen that don't seem fair. But we can trust God, no matter what we're going through. We can trust God even with the hard things."

"Like moving halfway across the world?" Chelsea Marie pouted.

"Well, Indiana is hardly halfway across the world," her grandmother said with a smile, "though it must feel like that when you're only nine years old. But yes, you can trust God, even with something that big. Did I ever tell you about the time I trusted God to heal me?"

Chelsea Marie's eyes widened. "No, ma'am. I don't think so." Surely she would have remembered that!

"Yes," Grand Doll said. "Many years ago, I was diagnosed with a heart problem."

Chelsea Marie clamped a hand over her mouth, startled. "I didn't know that!"

"Well, it's true," Grand Doll said. "My heart wasn't beating correctly, and I was a little discouraged, to be honest. But God gave me the faith to believe He could heal my heart. I trusted Him. I truly believed He would heal me."

"Did He?"

"Yes, and I remember the day it happened," Grand Doll said. "My faith was so strong! On that day, a warm breeze seemed to wrap itself around my entire body, and I just knew I had been healed." She turned to face Chelsea Marie. "From that day on my heart began to beat regularly. I went back to the doctor for a checkup, and I was fine."

"Wow!"

"Wow is right!" Grand Doll said. "It's been more than twenty years, and I am still healed, praise God! That's what trusting God will do for you!"

Chelsea Marie felt better after hearing Grand Doll's story. "Thank you for telling me that," she said. Maybe she *could* learn to trust God like her grandmother had done, even if it was really, really hard.

They walked along the trail together for several minutes looking at the leaves, the trees, and the rocks— talking about many things. After awhile, Grand Doll hummed a familiar tune with a beautiful melody line. Before long, they were both singing together: "*Trust and obey, for there's no other way to be happy in Jesus, but to trust and obey.*"

"I love that song," Grand Doll said.

"Me too," Chelsea Marie agreed.

"And the words are so true," Grand Doll added. "There really is no other way to be happy, outside of trusting God."

Chelsea Marie thought about that for a minute. "I learned a memory verse about trust." She quoted it for Grand Doll. "*Trust in the LORD with all thine heart; and lean not unto thine own understanding. In all thy ways acknowledge him, and he shall direct thy paths*, Proverbs 3:5-6."

"That's right," her grandmother said. "He *will* direct your paths, wherever you live, wherever you go, and whatever you do."

Just then, Chelsea Marie remembered the wagon wheel they had seen at the entrance of the trail. "Grand Doll…" She tugged on her grandmother's sleeve. "You said you would tell me a story—one about a wagon wheel. Will you tell it to me now?"

Grand Doll looked ahead at the trail and said, "Why, sure! It's part of a much bigger story and I know you will love it. Are you ready to hear a great adventure?"

"Yes ma'am."

"You will really have to listen closely, for this is an amazing story—one that took place long, long ago. And it's a story about a little girl you are related to."

"Really? What was her name?"

"Her name was Katie Sue," Grand Doll said with a nod, "and she went through a lot of changes in her life, just like you! She had to learn how to trust and obey, just like you're learning to do. Would you like to hear her story now?"

"Oh yes!" Chelsea Marie clapped her hands together. "Please tell me!"

And so, the story began…

"I love Tennessee in the fall," the
eleven-year-old whispered to herself.

A Beautiful Season

ROBERTSON COUNTY, TENNESSEE 1851

*K*ATIE SUE HEROD SKIPPED HAPPILY along behind her mother and her twin sisters on their way toward the house after their chores. She was careful not to spill her basket of eggs but soon grew distracted by the beauty around her. Overhead, the autumn leaves glistened red and gold, and she stopped for a moment to stare at them in wonder.

"I *love* Tennessee in the fall," the eleven-year-old whispered to herself.

She loved the way the colorful leaves looked as they tumbled from the trees, and she loved the way they smelled when Papa gathered them into piles after they'd turned brown. Most of all, she loved the way she felt every year as the lazy days of summer slipped into the chilly days of fall. Truly, there was no prettier place to enjoy the changing of the seasons than Robertson County, Tennessee—the place where she had been born and planned to spend the rest of her life.

"Hurry up, Katie Sue," her mother called out. "Papa's getting hungry. He will be arriving any moment now for lunch!"

"Yes ma'am." Katie Sue pulled her wool cape over her shoulders as the brisk October air sent a little shiver down her spine. She pushed a loose strand of blond hair out of her eyes, and then followed along behind her mother and little sisters, lost in thought. She could see the house off in the distance and knew Mama was in a hurry to prepare the noon meal for the family.

Soon Papa would take a break from his work and join them. There, he would eat, and kiss Katie Sue on the forehead, calling her "Duchess," like he always did because she was such a proper young lady. Afterwards, he would tell her and her sisters a funny story and take a short nap before heading back to work. No matter how busy he was, he always took time out for his afternoon nap on the sun porch, resting against one of the cane chairs.

Katie Sue loved her papa's stories, but today she had something else on her mind as well. Today, Mama had given her special permission to spend all afternoon with Matilda in town. Of all the things Katie Sue loved to do, spending time with her best friend was her very favorite.

The two girls loved their time together, playing hide-and-seek, checkers, fox and geese, and other fun games in the large two-story inn where Matilda lived with her parents and older brothers—not far from the Herod's farm. What fun they would have! She could hardly wait!

Papa arrived shortly, and everyone gathered around the table for a wonderful meal.

The twins bounced up and down with as much excitement as any six-year-olds could possibly have. "We missed you, Papa!" Lottie said.

"Do you have to go back to work after we eat?" Lucy said with a pout. "Can't you spend the afternoon playing with us?"

Papa gave them kisses on their foreheads and said, "There's too much work to be done at the cotton gin. You know it's the busy season for me. I only run the gin three to four months out of the year during the cotton harvest season. Perhaps this evening we can play a game or two. How would that be?"

They squealed their delight.

Katie Sue looked at her papa, thinking what a hard worker he was. He ran the cotton gin in town and also owned the blacksmith shop. She barely saw him during the busy cotton season because he spent most of his time at the gin. Then, he still had to oversee the blacksmith shop, and there was the family farm to take care of as well. She didn't know how he did it. Just thinking about it all was exhausting.

As the family ate, her papa told a story, just as Katie Sue knew he would. This one was an adventurous tale—about a fellow who traveled by wagon train all the way from Tennessee to Texas.

"What's a wagon train, Papa?" Lucy asked.

"A wagon train is a long line of wagons traveling together across the country. They cross mountains, prairies, and even raging rivers! They travel together because it is safer and smarter to travel in groups." He continued on with his story. Katie Sue's little sisters listened in awe, and so did Katie Sue, though the idea of crossing raging rivers certainly didn't sound like much fun to her.

Papa told the story with excitement in his voice and a twinkle in his eye. Truly, there was no better storyteller in all of Robertson County than James Herod—that was a fact.

"Sounds like quite a remarkable journey, doesn't it, Duchess?" her father asked as he finished.

Katie Sue thought about that for a minute and finally shrugged. "I suppose." To be honest, traveling in a wagon train didn't sound very nice to her at all. In fact, it sounded like a lot of trouble, and not very comfortable either. How would one keep her clothes clean, what with all the dust the wagon wheels and horses and mules would blow up?

Turning her attention to more pleasant things, she asked, "Would it be all right if I visited with Matilda now?" She could hardly wait to see her best friend.

"Yes, of course," Papa said with a wink. "Mama will be by to get you after she and the twins do their shopping. Be a good girl—and be sure to have fun!"

"Oh, I will," she promised. She always had fun when she and Matilda spent time together.

After helping her mama with the lunch dishes, the time arrived at last. Katie Sue and her mother walked briskly down the country road with the twins tagging along behind, picking up speed as they drew near the little town of White House. Katie Sue was careful not to soil her dress and to keep her curls in place, though it was a little hard with the twins roughhousing behind her all the way to town. Honestly, Katie Sue would never understand how the twins turned out to be such tomboys!

As always, the town was busy with people everywhere. The ladies looked so pretty in their full, ruffled skirts and paisley shawls. When she grew up, Katie Sue wanted to look just like them! The businessmen, with their thick moustaches and starched shirts, strolled about visiting with one another. The children ran around, laughing and playing.

"Look, Mama!" The twins squealed as they pointed at a stage coach filled with travelers.

"Perhaps one day we will travel," Mama said with a smile.

"Oh, can we?" Lucy asked with a sigh. "I want to go to Texas!"

"Me too!" Lottie agreed. "Let's go on a wagon train, just like the man in Papa's story!"

Katie Sue shrugged. As much fun as it was to watch people come and go, she was perfectly content to stay here—in Tennessee—forever. Traveling was fine for other people, but she preferred to stay put.

A short time later, Katie Sue, her mother, and the twins arrived at the beautiful White House Inn, where they were met at the door by Mrs. Wilks, Matilda's mother.

"Hannah, it's so nice to see you and your daughters," Mrs. Wilks said as she led them into the parlor.

"Thank you," Katie Sue's mother said as she tried to quiet down the twins.

"Welcome, Katie Sue," Mrs. Wilks said with a wide smile. "Is this a new dress you are wearing?"

"It is." Katie Sue beamed.

"Mrs. Anderson is a wonderful seamstress," Katie Sue's mother said with a nod. "I shall miss her terribly."

Katie Sue couldn't help but wonder what her mama meant. Was Mrs. Anderson moving away? How sad, to lose a good family friend and such a wonderful seamstress. Why, practically every woman in Robertson County went to Mrs. Anderson to have her dresses made. Whatever would they do without her?

"The handiwork on this skirt is very nice," Mrs. Wilks commented, "and I love the color of the bodice coat. It is very lovely." She gave Katie Sue a wink. "Give me a spin, so I can see the back of your dress."

Katie Sue twirled around in a circle and the skirt whipped around behind her.

"Looking at you in that beautiful dress makes me wish I were young and slender again." Mrs. Wilks put her hands on her broad hips and chuckled. "Those days are behind me now, but it's fun to see you girls looking so dainty."

"Oh, yes ma'am." Katie Sue loved dainty things— pretty dresses, lacy gloves, and such. She wished her twin sisters would stop mussing up their dresses with their tomboyish ways.

Mrs. Wilks nodded. "And that color of blue reminds me of the sky. You look especially lovely in it. It brings out the blue in your eyes."

"Thank you, ma'am." Katie Sue couldn't help but giggle. She loved her new dress, and would especially love showing it to her best friend for the first time.

"I would imagine you are aching to see Matilda," Mrs. Wilks said with a twinkle in her eye. "She is waiting for you up in her room."

"Yes ma'am."

"Now, behave yourself, Katie Sue," her mother said with a pretend stern look.

"Behave yourself, Sis!" Lottie and Lucy both said with a laugh.

Katie Sue smiled. Her little sisters were only six, but both of them knew how to make her smile. "Of course, I will behave!" she agreed. She kissed her mother good-bye, gave the girls a silly smile, and then ran up the stairs in search of her best friend. She arrived at Matilda's bedroom door completely out of breath but ready for fun.

"I thought you'd never get here!" Matilda said, as the door swung wide.

"Me neither," Katie Sue agreed, "but I'm here now. What do you think of my new dress?"

"Oh, it's very pretty," Matilda said, touching the fabric and admiring the lace that adorned the collar, sleeves, and hem.

"What shall we do first?" Katie Sue asked. "Checkers?"

"I don't feel like playing checkers today."

Katie Sue grinned, thinking about one of their favorite games. "Jacks, then," she suggested, "or perhaps pickup sticks?" She knew it was one of Matilda's favorites.

Matilda shook her head and then held up a large piece of paper with all sorts of squiggly lines drawn on it. "I've been looking at this all afternoon," she said.

"What is it?" Katie Sue asked.

"It's a map of the Louisiana Purchase. Our third president, Thomas Jefferson, purchased the entire territory from France in 1803 for only $15 million! My papa says we practically stole it for such a small price. See?" Matilda pointed. "Look how large it is. The famous explorers Lewis and Clark led an expedition to explore the territory. They started in Missouri and traveled west along the Missouri River and then northwest through the plains and then west again through the Oregon Territory all the way to the Pacific Ocean." She traced their route along the map with her finger. On and on she went, talking about the different places she hoped to see someday. Her face beamed with joy as she talked.

"You sound just like Papa," Katie Sue said with a shrug. "He likes to tell stories about traveling too."

"I really hope to travel someday," Matilda said with a dreamy look in her eyes. She went to the window and looked out onto the street below. "Sometimes I see all of the coaches coming and going, and I get a little jealous."

"You do?"

Matilda nodded. "Yes. I can't think of anything more fun that traveling to places I've never been before."

"And I can't think of anything worse," Katie Sue said with a laugh, "because traveling would mean I would have to leave you—and I could never do that!" She wrapped her best friend in a warm embrace, and before long they were playing together—all stories about traveling far behind them.

---

*"Papa, do you mean to say that
we are going to leave Tennessee
and travel to Texas...to live?"*

SURPRISING NEWS

ATIE SUE RETURNED HOME WITH MAMA
and the twins, tired but happy after a
long afternoon of playing with Matilda.
Mama went off to the kitchen to prepare dinner, and
Lottie and Lucy headed off to play in their bedroom.
Katie Sue looked around for Papa and finally found him
in the parlor, gazing at a large map.

He turned as she came in the room, and gave her a
little wink. As she drew close, she noticed a twinkle in
his eye. Her father always got a twinkle in his eye when
he was about to play a prank. Perhaps that's what he had
in store for her now.

"Duchess, I'd like to talk with you for a minute." He
sat in a chair and patted his knee—a signal for Katie Sue
to join him.

"Yes sir." She sat upon his knee and waited—for what,
she wasn't sure.

"Do you remember that story I told you earlier—about the man traveling in the wagon train?" He stared into her eyes with a very serious look upon his face.

"Of course, Papa." She nodded, but couldn't help but wonder why he would tell the same story all over again.

"The man in that story was me," he said.

"W…what?" That didn't make any sense at all. Why, Papa had never traveled to Texas, had he? "I'm not sure I understand," she said, her brows knit in confusion.

"I told you that story earlier to make you understand…"

"Understand what, Papa?"

"To make you understand that we, the Herod family, the whole lot of us—are going to Texas!"

Katie Sue was so surprised, she almost fell off of her father's knee. Surely she had heard wrong. "Papa, do you mean to say that we are going to *leave* Tennessee and travel to Texas…to *live*?"

"Yes, Duchess." He smiled the happiest smile she had ever seen, but Katie Sue certainly didn't feel like smiling. In fact, she didn't know if she would ever smile again. She couldn't imagine leaving Robertson County. Not ever.

"But, Papa…" She shook her head and fought back the tears. "What about Matilda? What about my school?" A lump rose up in her throat and she tried to push it down, but could not.

"I know it will be sad to leave your school and your best friend," her father explained, "but there will be a school in Texas and you will meet many wonderful girls on the wagon train. Several families will be traveling together—folks from all over this part of Tennessee, in fact."

"But…, Papa!"

"Just wait, Katie Sue." Mama's happy voice rang out as she approached with an apron tied about her waist. "When we arrive in Texas, you will meet all sorts of new people."

Her mother's eyes were filled with excitement as she spoke, just like Papa's. Surely *she* wasn't happy about this. Why, Mama loved Tennessee!

Katie Sue suddenly realized what Mama had been talking about earlier. Mrs. Anderson, the seamstress, wasn't going anywhere. *She*—Katherine Susannah Herod—was going somewhere, but she didn't want to. Not now, not ever. Why, the very idea broke her heart!

Papa's voice took on a serious tone as he continued. "Katie Sue, you're old enough to understand this now. Do you remember reading 'The Great Commission' in the Bible?"

"Yes sir." She quoted it from memory. " '*Go ye therefore, and teach all nations, baptizing them in the name of the Father, and of the Son, and of the Holy Ghost*,' Matthew 28:19."

"What was that first word, again?" her father asked with the twinkle returning to his eye.

She thought about it a moment, then said, "Go?"

"That's right." He grinned with delight. "The Lord is calling us to go to places we've never been before. I believe with all my heart the Herod family is supposed to go to Texas to make disciples. Texas is a brand new state, and there are plenty of folks there needing to hear the Gospel. Think of all the people who don't even know about our Lord and Savior, Jesus Christ, and we can go and share the Good News with them."

Katie Sue thought about that for a moment. How could she complain, when Papa made it all sound so wonderful? And yet, how could she leave her home, her school, and her best friend in all the world? Why, her heart ached, just thinking about it.

"Many from Tennessee have already gone to Texas," Katie Sue's mother explained. "In fact, some of our own brave men fought at the Alamo. Do you remember hearing about that?"

"Yes. I remember hearing the story of Davy Crockett," she said. "He died in the battle at the Alamo, isn't that right?"

"Yes. He was a very brave Tennessean who gave his life for his friends in Texas," Papa said. "And even though Texas did not win its independence from Mexico that day at the Battle of the Alamo, the men fought bravely, giving their lives for the cause of freedom. There were around 200 men who fought at the Alamo, and all of them died. 'Remember the Alamo' became the battle cry that swept through Texas. Later, at the battle of San Jacinto on April 21, 1836, Sam Houston defeated Santa Anna and Texas finally gained its freedom from Mexico."

A little shiver went down Katie Sue's arms. It all sounded dreadful to her. In fact, most everything about Texas sounded a little scary and wild. Papa had told the story of the Alamo many times over. But in the other stories he told, Texas sounded like a frightening place— a wilderness not yet settled, a savage land filled with all sorts of people who spoke different languages and fought with one another. Why, Texas had only been a state for a few years. Surely he wouldn't take them there. Why, he couldn't! Could he?

"When we get to Texas," Papa continued, "we will start a new church."

"A new church?" She could hardly imagine attending church in a new place. She loved her church right here in Robertson County.

Though she tried not to let the tears come, they came anyway. Before long, Katie Sue was swiping at her eyes. She didn't say a word. She wouldn't dare. If she spoke, she might let her parents know how she felt—how she *really* felt.

"I know this news is hard to take," Papa said, "but you're a big girl, Katie Sue—big enough to understand that the Lord is calling us to a new place, a new people."

"We're going to Texas!" Lottie and Lucy squealed in unison as they entered the room jumping up and down in excitement.

"But I don't want to be with new people," Katie Sue whispered. "I like the old ones just fine."

Papa stared deep into her eyes as he asked a question. "Do you trust me, Daughter?"

"O…of course."

"Have I ever given you reason not to?"

"No sir."

Her father gestured for her to stand alongside him. "Then you must trust me now. And more importantly, you must trust the Lord, for He is the One who gave me the idea to move to Texas in the first place."

"H…He did?"

"Yes." Papa looked up to the sky and brought his hands together as if he were praying. "And when the Lord speaks, we must listen."

"Do you remember that Bible verse we memorized last week?" Mama asked.

"W…which one?" Katie Sue wiped her nose with the back of her hand and sniffled.

"The one from Proverbs 3:5-6," Mama said. "*Trust in the* LORD *with all thine heart; and lean not unto thine own understanding. In all thy ways acknowledge him, and he shall direct thy paths."*

Katie Sue nodded her head. "Yes ma'am. I remember now."

"God promises to make our paths straight if we trust in Him with all of our hearts," Papa explained. "That means He will tell us the right way to go. Trusting Him is the most important thing of all, though it isn't always easy."

"Katie Sue…" Her mother reached to take her hand. "Just think of the adventures that lie ahead. Think of what it will be like as we travel on the wagon train with so many other families. Think about the wonderful times we will have, and all of the memories we will make together."

Right now, Katie Sue couldn't imagine—even for one teeny-tiny moment—how she could possibly make any memories without Matilda in them. How in the world would she get over the ache in her heart, every time she thought of leaving? And…to ride on a dusty, dirty wagon train all the way to Texas? She could hardly believe it!

Then again… She gazed up into her Papa's excited eyes, knowing she could not complain. How could she, when he was trusting God with their future?

Whether she liked it or not, Katie Sue had to face the truth. Her family was moving to Texas…and she was going with them.

"But most of all, I will miss you. I think I could manage traveling all the way to Texas if you were coming too."

WANTING TO STAY

*E*ARLY THE NEXT MORNING, THE HEROD family awoke, ate breakfast and dressed for church. Katie Sue dressed very slowly, not paying a bit of attention to the buttons on her bodice as she fastened them. After a minute or so, she looked down and let out a groan, realizing she'd buttoned them wrong. But who could blame her? She had hardly slept a wink all night. She'd spent much of the night with her face buried in the pillow, crying silent tears. She didn't want her mama and her papa to know, but her heart was broken.

With a sigh, she unbuttoned the bodice and started all over again. Doing so reminded her of her life. She was about to have to start all over again, though she didn't want to. No, she wanted things to stay just as they were.

Some time later, as the family approached the familiar wood-framed church building, Katie Sue looked around for Matilda. She had to tell her best friend the news—right away.

Sadly, she didn't get a chance, at least not at first. A group of chattering women gathered around the Herod family as they got out of their wagon and began to ask question after question.

"I hear you are moving to Texas!" Mrs. Gertsch, the pastor's wife, said. She clutched Mama's hand. "We will miss you so!"

"Indeed." Mama's eyes watered. "We will miss you all too. But we believe the Lord is leading us to Texas to spread the Gospel, and we must go where He leads."

"Of course." Mrs. Gertsch reached to give her a kiss on the cheek. "You will win many to the Lord, I feel sure."

Mrs. Anderson, the seamstress, wrapped her arms around Mama. "I shall miss sewing for you and your wonderful family." The older woman turned to give Katie Sue a sad smile. "I feel so blessed to have had you as customers and friends."

"Don't say good-bye to us just yet," Mama said with a smile. "We will need some sturdy traveling clothes, so the girls and I will visit you at your shop later this week. My husband will come a few days later, as he will need new trousers and shirts. You will have plenty of time to fill the order. We hope to leave by the early spring, as soon as the snow thaws."

"I feel certain I can accommodate you," Mrs. Anderson said. "It seems I've been sewing more than my share of traveling clothes these days. Many folks from

Tennessee seem to be heading west." She dabbed at her eyes. "Makes me sad, to be sure."

"Westward, ho!" Mrs. Gertsch bellowed. "That's the phrase I've been hearing for months! Folks from all over the East Coast are heading west in search of new lives!"

"Indeed," Mama said with a smile.

"True, true," Mrs. Anderson echoed. After a minute, a twinkle lit her eyes. "But I will stay put in Robertson County. Why, with all of the traveling clothes needed, my business will continue to grow."

As the women began to talk about what sort of clothing items the family would need for the trip, Katie Sue broke through the crowd in search of Matilda. She found her best friend inside the church, sitting in the back pew with the saddest look on her face she had ever seen.

"You've heard, haven't you?" Katie Sue sat next to her with a sigh.

Matilda nodded but didn't say anything. Katie Sue slipped an arm around her friend's shoulder, and they sat in silence for a moment.

"I will miss Tennessee so much," Katie Sue said, finally. "I will miss the sound of the wind whipping through the trees in the fall, knocking all the leaves to the ground. It always sounds like music to me."

"Me too," Matilda whispered.

"And the leaves are like a beautiful painting." Katie Sue let out a long sigh. "I will miss the mountains…" Her voice faded as she thought about the beautiful mountains around her home—brilliantly green in the summertime, and faded to brown in the early winter before the snows hit. "I will miss my house and the school." Katie Sue turned to face her best friend, and grabbed her hand as she finished. "But most of all, I will miss *you*. I think I could manage traveling all the way to Texas if you were coming too."

"I *want* to come." Matilda looked at her with tears streaming down her face. "Don't you see? I want to travel."

At once, Katie Sue saw the dilemma. *Of course.* Her best friend longed to travel. Why, she had said so, just yesterday. She—Katie Sue—longed to stay put. If only they could trade places! But, then again, if Matilda moved away, they would still be apart. That wouldn't solve a thing!

"Can't you just pack me in your trunk?" Matilda whispered, her voice quite serious.

"W…what?" Katie Sue couldn't tell if her best friend was teasing or not.

"I wouldn't be a bother, I promise. And I don't eat much. You could just sneak a few bites of food to me every now and again."

Katie Sue couldn't help but laugh aloud at that image. Just the thought of Matilda packed away in a trunk made her giggle.

The others began to take their seats, and before she knew it, the hymn singing had begun. As the others around her sang out with great joy, Katie Sue found herself lost in her thoughts. She couldn't even pretend to be happy about moving so far away.

Finally, Pastor Gertsch took his place behind the pulpit and began to preach. Sometimes his sermons were a little long, but today Katie Sue paid attention, for today he was speaking on a topic near to her heart.

"I would like to start with a few scriptures from the Psalms," the pastor said, as he opened his large black Bible. As he read the words from Psalm 37:5 aloud, Katie Sue found herself paying close attention. "*Commit thy way unto the LORD,*" the pastor read. "*Trust also in him; and he shall bring it to pass.*"

The pastor then turned to Psalm 33:21 and read, "*For our heart shall rejoice in him, because we have trusted in his holy name.*"

His next passage was from Proverbs 3:5-6. "*Trust in the LORD with all thine heart; and lean not unto thine own understanding,*" he read in a booming voice. "*In all thy ways acknowledge him, and he shall direct thy paths.*"

"Oh my goodness," Katie Sue whispered. Why, that was the very scripture her mama and her papa had used just yesterday. Was the Lord trying to tell her something? To trust in Him completely, perhaps? To trust that He would direct her path? Even all the way to Texas?

After the service ended, several of the Herod's friends gathered around once again to get the details. This time, Papa did most of the talking. With a gleam in his eyes and a broad smile on his face, he told everyone about what it would be like to travel by wagon train to Texas.

"This will be the adventure of a lifetime!" he said with a smile. "Truly, the adventure of a lifetime."

As they pulled away from the church awhile later, Katie Sue thought about what he had said. Yes, she was about to set out on an adventure; that was for sure. But even so, traveling all the way to Texas sure didn't feel like much fun. She wondered if it ever would.

She held up a bolt of rather dull-looking brown print fabric, and Katie Sue frowned.

TRAVELING CLOTHES

*T*HE WEEK BEFORE THANKSGIVING, Mama and all the girls took the wagon to town to visit with Mrs. Henderson at the dress shop. Though she wasn't happy about traveling to Texas, Katie Sue was tickled to be getting new clothes. She loved pretty dresses and hoped Mama would allow her to have one more made up in cornflower blue, her favorite color. One could never have too many blue dresses, after all.

They arrived in town and the twins begged to go to the mercantile to purchase some lemon drops. Mama promised that if they behaved at Mrs. Henderson's, she would consider it. Katie Sue doubted they would truly behave. They were often a bit rowdy, especially while being fitted for dresses.

Katie Sue shivered underneath the quilt her mama had put in the wagon. She could hardly believe Thanksgiving was almost here. Christmas would be next, and then New

Year's. Then…she didn't want to think about the spring coming. No, when the spring came, they would have to leave—have to go to Texas. She closed her eyes and tried not to think about it.

A short time later, they arrived at Mrs. Henderson's. The happy-go-lucky woman met them at the door of her shop with a huge smile and a loud, "Welcome, Herod family!" She ushered them inside and offered them hot apple cider. "To take the chill off," she explained. After they drank their cider, it was time to start talking about the clothes she would make.

"Hannah, let me show you and the girls some dress patterns," Mrs. Henderson said. She pulled open a catalogue and everyone gathered around.

Katie Sue sighed with delight as she looked at lovely pictures of girls in frilly dresses with lace and ruffles. "I want one like this," she said, pointing to a delightful dress with the loveliest lace collar she had ever seen.

Mama chuckled. "Well, I'm sure you would look pretty in a dress like that, sweetheart, but we're here to purchase traveling clothes. They must be practical. No frills. And they will not be made of silk like the dress in that picture, I assure you."

Katie Sue let out a sigh.

"Calico is a very popular fabric for traveling clothes," Mrs. Henderson explained. She held up a bolt of rather dull-looking brown print fabric, and Katie Sue frowned.

She didn't like it at all, and couldn't imagine traveling across the country in anything so dreary.

"See, Katie Sue..." Mama reached out to touch the fabric. "It's soft but sturdy. Perfect for traveling."

"And it sews up nicely," Mrs. Henderson added. "Especially for traveling clothes, when skirts need to be full to keep away the insects and such."

Katie shuddered at the word insects, then glanced at the dreary fabric once more. "But it's so. . .so. . ." She didn't finish her sentence for fear of hurting feelings.

"Still, this is what we will be choosing," Mama said. "Practicality is most important when traveling, from the top of your head to the soles of your feet."

"The top of my head?" Katie Sue reached up to touch her curls. "What do you mean?"

"I mean you will wear braids for the journey," Mama said, "and no arguments about it."

Katie Sue did her best not to argue, though she much preferred curls to braids. But, to think that she had to wear a drab brown dress *and* braids? It sounded dreadful.

"You will find that comfort will be very important," Mama added, "so no fretting."

Mrs. Henderson's face lit in a smile. "Come now, ladies," she said. "It is time to select your fabric colors, and I have plenty to choose from. Come with me." Everyone followed along behind her to the back of the shop where they saw bolts and bolts of fabric. "Here are the calicos," Mrs. Henderson said, pointing to a large stack.

Katie Sue's eyes widened. "Ooo!" Perhaps this wouldn't be as difficult as she'd feared. There were plenty of lovely colors here. Right away, she eyed a lovely shade of blue. The print was quite pretty, and she hoped Mama would allow her to choose it.

Sure enough, Mama gave her approval. "You always look beautiful in blue, Katie Sue," her mother said, "because it brings out the blue in your eyes!"

"Does that mean we have to get brown dresses?" Lottie pouted. "Just 'cause our eyes are brown like Papa's?"

"No, my dear," Mother said with a smile. "I was thinking of green for the two of you. How would that be?"

"Ooo, green!" Lucy squealed. "I love green."

"Me too!" Lottie agreed.

The twins took to chattering about their dresses while Mrs. Henderson went to work, taking measurements.

"I must say, you are getting tall, Katie Sue," she said. "I will have to make this dress a good inch and a half longer than the last one."

Katie Sue stood up straight and smiled. "Yes ma'am, I feel taller." She envisioned herself in the blue calico dress with her blond hair pulled back in braids. Perhaps she wouldn't look too dreary. She could tie some pretty blue ribbons at the end of her braids. Oh, but if only she could have a lace collar like the girl in the picture!

Just then, Katie Sue's mama appeared at her side with a bolt of lace in her hands. "What about this lovely white lace to add to the collar of Katie's Sue's blue dress?" she asked. "I think it would make the dress even prettier."

"Oh, Mama, really?" Katie Sue squealed. "I love it!"

"I thought it might be a lovely surprise," Mama said with a smile.

"Oh, I love you, Mama!" Katie Sue said with a grin.

The twins giggled, and then Mrs. Henderson grinned. "You girls always put a smile on my face."

After all the selections had been made, Mama ordered some bonnets and shawls, and then she and Mrs. Henderson began to talk about the one thing Katie Sue was trying *not* to think about.

"So, when will you be leaving?" Mrs. Henderson asked.

"Early spring, as soon as the roads are clear," Mama explained. "James is quite set on the idea of arriving in Texas before the summer so that he can plant his first crop and begin work on the church."

"Is that what he will do in Texas, then?" Mrs. Henderson asked. "Farm?"

"Yes, and preach," Mama explained.

"He is an excellent Bible teacher, to be sure," Mrs. Henderson said. "Why, I love it when he speaks in Pastor Gertsch's absence."

"He enjoys telling others about the Lord," Mama said with a smile, "and that's why we are going to Texas. He wants to plant churches—not just one, but several."

Katie Sue's ears perked up. Several churches? Not just one? This was the first time she'd heard of this news.

"We're meeting up with some folks in Texas named Powell," Mama said. "One of the boys, not yet twenty, is a teacher. He will help build the school, which we will also use as a church. But over time, James hopes to plant half a dozen churches."

"Sounds like quite an adventure," replied Mrs. Henderson. "But what about James's cotton gin and his blacksmithing business?"

Mama sighed. "It's sad, I know, but he is selling the cotton gin and the blacksmithing business to fund our trip. It was a hard decision, to be sure. We truly believe the Lord will meet all of our needs if we are faithful, so I'm not worried."

"Still," Mrs. Henderson had a worried look in her eye as she spoke, "Texas is a rugged place. I do hope you fare well there."

Mama reached out and squeezed her friend's hand. "We will do better than that," she said. "We will live a good life in Texas. I know it because as I've prayed, the Lord has given me a real peace about moving."

Peace? Katie Sue thought about that. She hadn't thought to pray about the move yet. If she prayed, would God give her a peace too?

Later, as they traveled home together in the wagon, Katie Sue closed her eyes and offered up a prayer. "*Lord,*" she whispered, "*You know that I don't want to go to Texas. Please help me through this. I need peace, just like Mama has. I am putting my trust in You, Lord.*"

By the time she opened her eyes again, she felt a little better about the journey ahead.

Finally, when the time had come, friends gathered around from far and near to say their good-byes to the Herod family.

LEAVING HOME

*K*ATIE SUE PRAYED FOR A LONG, LONG winter so that she would have more time to spend with Matilda. But, in spite of her best wishes, spring came early to Robertson County that year. In early March, the snows thawed and the roads were cleared for travel. Her heart ached as she thought about leaving, but there was no turning back now.

Papa loaded the long, boatlike covered wagon, which he called a Conestoga, with all of their personal belongings. He took great care to pack everything of value to the family inside. The twins worked alongside him, helping load the smaller items. Their adorable brown braids bounced up and down as they worked. As Katie Sue watched, she could hardly believe they could fit so much in the wagon.

Katie Sue's curiosity got the best of her. She climbed up on one of the big spoke wheels and peeked inside.

"It is bigger than it looks!" She crawled on in for a look around. The wagon was filled with their clothing, furniture, the highboy, and even the harpsichord. Pots and pans, as well as milk cans and weapons, hung on hooks from the wooden bows overhead. Why, Katie Sue could hardly believe they could fit so much inside and still have room to travel, but there appeared to be just enough space.

She settled back against the quilts and other bedcovers Mama had spread out on the floorboard and glanced up at the oak bows overhead with the canvas stretched tight over them. What if a storm blew up as they were traveling? Would this fabric ceiling be enough to protect them? Papa had rubbed the canvas down with oil to seal it, but would that really help, as he'd said? A little shiver ran up her spine as she thought about it. How frightening it would be to sleep in such a place during a thunderstorm!

"Katie Sue, where are you?"

She scrambled over the edge of the wagon and down to the ground below as she heard her mother's voice.

"Come on, my dear," her mother said. "We still have much to do."

Katie Sue followed her mama back into the house, where they cleaned it from top to bottom. One of the families from in town—the Trowbridge family—had purchased it from Papa. Katie Sue could hardly stand the thought of someone else living in her house, sleeping in her room, but she must. And how sad, to think that Papa had to sell his cotton gin and the blacksmith business. Things were changing, and there was nothing she could do about it.

Still, he hadn't seemed sad at all. In fact, he had seemed almost happy about it. "Whenever you sell out for God," Papa had said, "He always makes it up to you!"

Katie Sue couldn't help but admire Papa. He trusted in God, to be sure. She prayed that she would have that same kind of trust as well.

Finally, when the time had come, friends gathered around from far and near to say their good-byes to the Herod family.

"We will miss you terribly," Mrs. Gertsch said with tears in her eyes. "Church services just won't be the same without the Herod family." She turned to face Katie Sue's mama. "We will miss your beautiful singing voice, Hannah."

"Yes, we shall. But we are very proud of you," Reverend Gertsch was quick to add. "You are following the leading of the Lord, traveling to a new place to spread the Gospel message. There is no greater calling."

"No greater calling." Katie Sue whispered the words. Was Reverend Gertsch right? Was this journey part of God's call on her life? She looked over into Matilda's tear-filled eyes and started crying right away. She wrapped her arms around her best friend's neck, and they whispered their good-byes.

Just as they pulled apart, her father slipped something into her hand.

"What is this, Papa?" She looked down to discover a lovely gold locket about the size of a large coin. On the top of the locket, two tiny gold friendship birds stood beak to beak. On the bottom of the locket were three small diamond chips. "Oh, Papa!" She stared at the beautiful keepsake, unable to say anything else.

"We had this made for you, Duchess," he said with a wink, "to remember Matilda. Open the locket, if you please."

She gingerly pried it open, amazed to find two tiny photographs inside—hers and Matilda's. She recognized the photo of herself, of course. Mr. Mullins had taken it last spring, but the photograph of Matilda was new.

"How did you do this?" she asked in amazement.

"Mr. Mullins took my photograph at Christmastime," Matilda said with a smile. "I didn't want you to see it till now." She leaned in and the two girls looked at the locket together. "This way, you will never forget me," Matilda whispered.

Katie Sue clutched the precious gold keepsake in her hand and wept. "I would never have forgotten you. I promise. But having this locket will make things easier.

Every time I feel lonely, I will open it and see your smiling face!"

It wasn't quite the same as packing Matilda away in her trunk and taking her along on the journey—but it was close.

Papa then handed Katie Sue a small book. "A diary," he explained, "so that you can write down the things you see in our travels."

She clutched the little book in her hand and looked up at her papa with tears in her eyes. "Thank you so much," she whispered. Perhaps this would ease the pain of leaving—to be able to write down her thoughts along the way.

"You're welcome, Duchess." He gave her a kiss on the forehead.

The men continued to load the wagon with one final item—Mama's large black trunk. It still had the sticker on the side from when her parents had traveled to Tennessee when Mama was just a girl.

Katie Sue gazed at the trunk and a smile lit her face as she remembered what Matilda had said: *"Can't you just pack me in your trunk? I wouldn't be a bother, I promise."*

"Oh, if only I could pack you inside," Katie Sue whispered to her best friend now. "I would take you with me, and we would be together…always!"

"We must learn to be happy, even though we are apart," Matilda said bravely.

Katie Sue thought about those words for a minute. Yes, Matilda was right. They must try. What else could they do? Still, the thought of packing her friend in the trunk seemed like a fun idea!

Mother patted the large black memory trunk and then turned to the others with a smile. "We will need to take special care of this," she said with a proud look in her eyes. "It's been in our family for over two hundred years. Came all the way over from Wales to London, and then across the Atlantic on a big ship, all the way to Virginia!"

"Goodness gracious!" Katie Sue thought about that. Two hundred years old? Perhaps one day she would own the trunk, and would pass it down to her children.

Still, knowing it was filled with the family's possessions—and knowing those possessions were traveling all the way to Texas—made her a bit sad.

Finally, the moment came. They could wait no longer.

"We must leave now," Papa announced. "We'll be joining the other wagons on the south end of town, just beyond the inn. We will travel together to the edge of Robertson County and camp out for the night with the others in the wagon train, then we will be on our way in the morning. That's when the real adventure will begin!"

Before the family loaded into the wagon, Papa made a final check to make sure everything was ready. He went to his new team of mules, checking and securing their harnesses. Katie Sue knew he was proud of his six new mules, saying they were "sure-footed, strong, and sturdy" for the long journey. Katie Sue would have much preferred a team of beautiful horses, but Papa explained that horses couldn't pull such a heavy load all the way to Texas.

With tears now flowing, the whole family climbed aboard the wagon. Katie Sue sat inside, underneath the covered top, with the twins nearby bouncing up and down in excitement. Mama and Papa sat up front. Papa grabbed ahold of the reins, and the wagon jolted as the mules pulled forward, causing the pots and pans to rattle against each other. Katie Sue almost toppled over, but quickly steadied herself.

"I don't think I can bear this," she whispered to her little sisters.

"Oh, Sis!" Lottie said with a laugh. "We're going to have an adventure!"

"Yes," Lucy echoed. "The time of our lives!"

"I don't want to have the time of my life," Katie Sue answered. "I just want to be with my friend. I want to stay here!"

As they pulled away, Katie Sue leaned out of the opening at the back of the wagon and waved at Matilda until she couldn't see her anymore. When her friend's face faded away in the distance, Katie Sue leaned back against the side of the wagon and wept. She clutched the tiny locket in her hand all the while, finally opening it to gaze at Matilda's face.

"I will miss you, my friend," she whispered. "I will miss you so very much."

The wagon bumped along through town and well beyond, and finally came to a clearing on the south end of the county. There, Katie Sue saw the most amazing sight! Wagons—dozens of them—lined up in rows. People, young and old, stood alongside them. Children in traveling clothes. Men with maps in their hands. Women, holding babies on their hips. Katie Sue had never seen so many adventurers all together in one place before. Her eyes could scarcely take in everything at once.

She looked around in amazement, noticing all of the animals as well. There were teams of oxen and mules to pull the wagons and horses for those who traveled on horseback. She also saw many dogs, some running around loose but most of them tied to the wagons.

And the smell! Why, the scent of the animals made her reach for a handkerchief and put it to her nose. "Oh, it's awful, Mama!" she cried. "How will we ever stand it?"

And the sounds! All around dogs barked, men talked, women soothed cranky children, and babies cried. Katie Sue felt completely overwhelmed.

As their wagon came to a stop, the twins quickly clamored out, excited to meet the others and help Papa. Though she didn't feel like facing anyone, Katie Sue finally climbed out of the wagon and stretched her legs. Right away, a couple of girls about her age approached and introduced themselves.

She met a happy-go-lucky girl with red hair named Peggy, who looked to be a lot of fun. Another girl named Josie looked a bit more standoffish. Her beautiful dark hair hung in perfect ringlets down her back. Katie Sue was a little envious because that was how she loved to wear her own hair. She had always received lots of compliments on her blond ringlets. Now her hair hung in two long braids down her front. She also admired Josie's stylish brocade dress. It was unlike anything Katie Sue had ever seen. Such finery! Why, she dreamed of having dresses like that. She glanced down at her own blue calico.

Then again, why would she need such a lovely dress in the wilds of Texas? She sighed and tried to put the thought out of her mind.

The womenfolk quickly put together a campfire and began to fix a meal for the crowd. The whole group of them ate together, and then the men met together to discuss the journey ahead.

All the while, Katie Sue clutched the locket in her hand and thought about Matilda. In fact, she had to wonder if she would ever stop thinking about her. No matter how long this trip turned out to be, it would seem even longer without her best friend's hand in her own.

March 9, 1851

Dear Diary,

The journey has begun. Tomorrow morning I will say good-bye to Robertson County forever. My heart is breaking. I will probably never see my best friend again. There are so many things I will miss—but mostly I will miss the beautiful mountains: the lush green of summer, the beautiful colors of fall, and the snowcapped peaks of winter. I will miss the rivers and streams as well. No matter where we travel, there will never be a place as pretty as my home... Tennessee.

Sincerely,
Katie Sue

*Traveling to Texas was turning out to be
a lot more fun than she had imagined,
and she was meeting new people,
just as Mama and Papa had said.*

ALONG THE TRAIL

HE NEXT MORNING, BEFORE THE SUN even peeked up from the eastern sky, folks were already busy. After eating an early breakfast, they gathered the livestock and lined up the wagons, one in front of the other. As far as the eye could see, people scurried about, loading up and preparing to head out West. Katie Sue did her best not to stare at the people around her, but it was hard.

Most of the womenfolk reminded her of Mama in nearly every way. They wore the same style bonnets and calico dresses. They worked hard to feed their families and tend to their children.

But many of the menfolk were *very* different from Papa. Some smelled of foul-smelling cigar smoke, and a few even forgot to tip their hats when a lady walked by. Gracious! Papa would never approve of that. On top of that, a few of the men driving the front wagons even looked and smelled as if they hadn't bathed in awhile. A little shiver ran down Katie Sue's spine as she thought about that. Was she going to get to bathe along the trail? She hoped so!

Most of the children seemed shy at first, several of the littler ones hiding behind their mothers' skirts. But after awhile, the boys started talking to one another, even laughing together. The little girls were very taken with the twins, especially in their identical green calico dresses and long brown braids with ribbons tied on the end.

The whole group of travelers was quite an amazing sight to behold. The wagons—most of them Conestogas, like the one Katie Sue's family drove—were hitched to large teams of mules or oxen. There were some smaller wagons as well but all had the same large canvas top. The smell of the animals—still not a pleasant odor—lingered in the air. So did the scent of coffee and bacon, which made the animal smell almost bearable.

Papa gathered the family together to tell them about their journey. "We will leave Robertson County through Nashville and head southwest for Memphis," he explained, pointing to a map.

"I've never been to Memphis before, Papa!" Lucy said.

"Nor I!" Lottie added.

"What happens after we reach Memphis?" Katie Sue asked.

"From there…," he pointed to the map, "we will cross the great Mississippi River into the state of Arkansas."

"Arkansas." Katie Sue whispered the word. She could hardly imagine being in a different state. What would it be like? Would it be different from Tennessee?

"Then what?" Lucy asked impatiently.

Papa continued to trace the map with his finger. "Then we will travel all the way across the state of Arkansas to a town called Little Rock where we will likely camp a few days. Little Rock is the capital of Arkansas. After that, we will head to the border of Texas."

"Texas!" both of the twins squealed in unison.

"At the Texas border, we will cross the Red River and likely set up camp again."

"Is the Red River really red, Papa?" Katie Sue asked.

Papa grinned. "We will see when we get there, Duchess!"

Katie Sue let out a sigh. She didn't want to see the Red River. She didn't want to travel all the way to Texas. She just wanted to stay in Tennessee.

"What happens after we get into Texas, Papa?" Lucy asked.

He pointed to the map one last time. "We will travel southwest to central Texas, to a place called Springfield where we will build our new home."

A smile lit his face as he talked, but Katie Sue didn't feel like smiling. The journey didn't look long when Papa traced it out on his map, but she guessed it would be weeks and weeks before they arrived at their new home.

Still, she did her best not to complain. She would endure this, no matter what.

Mama clapped her hands together. "Let's get on the road to Texas!"

"Anything you say, Mrs. Herod," Papa said with a wink. "Anything you say."

The whole family climbed aboard their wagon, which Papa had jokingly named Herod House. He took his place on the small wooden seat up front, and Mama joined him, looking about in every direction, and sweeping loose hairs under her bonnet with her fingertips.

Within minutes, every wagon in the line was moving. They were on their way! Katie Sue peeked out of the front of the wagon, smiling as she gazed out on the long line of wagons in front of them. She thought the sight of all those wagons with their canvas tops resembled ships sailing along over the ocean.

"So many!" She counted them. "One, two, three..." She finally stopped when she reached thirty-three. "Thirty-three wagons!" she proclaimed loudly, to be heard above the noise of the rattling wagon. Truly, she had never seen so many in one place before.

"A wagon *train*," Papa called back. "That's what they call it when so many travel together. And our wagon boss...," he gestured off in the distance to a fellow on horseback at the front of the line, "is Mr. McClintock. He rides on horseback so he can travel up and down the wagon train, making sure everything is in order. He's made this journey many times before, so we will arrive safe and sound, with his help."

"I like the sound of that," Mama said with a smile. "Safe and sound."

"Most of those other men on horseback are scouts. They ride ahead of the train, checking for danger as well as finding the best campsites and making sure there is water for us and the animals. They will also hunt wild game so we will have plenty to eat on the trail."

Papa held the reins in his hands, snapping them every few minutes to keep the team moving. "This wagon was built for journeys such as this," he explained. "It's sturdy, to be sure!" He gestured for Katie Sue to join them on the seat, and she scrambled to squeeze in between her parents, listening as Papa talked. "Did you know the Conestoga wagon can carry several thousand pounds of cargo?" he said.

"Several *thousand*?" Mama repeated.

"Goodness gracious!" Katie Sue thought about what Papa had said. Perhaps the wagon could withstand such a heavy load, but how could their poor mules pull so much weight? Why, the wagon held all of their family possessions, as well as large wooden buckets of water for the journey ahead. She couldn't imagine how the mules managed. "Poor animals," she said with a sigh. "I wouldn't want to pull such a load!"

"I hear tell one mule or ox can pull over a thousand pounds," Papa said, "but two…" He smiled. "Now two can pull several thousand. That's why it's best to travel with teams of four to six. You can get more done!"

"Still," Katie Sue said, "pulling a wagon all the way to Texas doesn't sound like much fun, even for a mule or an ox!"

"And walking all the way to Texas!" Mama said with a laugh. "I do not envy the animals, to be sure."

Papa let out a chuckle that bounced across the front of the wagon. "Mark my words," he said with a grin, "you will not feel like riding for long. Your backside will grow sore on this wooden seat, if you sit upon it all day long with the wagon bobbing up and down. You will want to walk much of the time as we travel along. In fact, you might envy the mules before long!"

Katie Sue thought about that for a moment before responding. "I don't mind walking alongside the wagon," she said, "as long as the weather is good."

"I hope our shoes hold out," Mama said with a wink.

"Just like the Israelites in the desert," Papa said, referring to the Bible story about Moses and the Israelites Katie Sue loved. "Our shoes will last all the way to Texas!"

"I've always loved that story," Mama added. "The Israelites, led by Moses, traveled across the desert for forty years to get to the Promised Land. God promised them that their shoes and clothes would not wear out until they reached the Promised Land, and God kept his promise."

"Forty years?" Katie Sue whispered. "Goodness." Traveling to Texas surely wouldn't take *that* long. She hoped not, anyway.

"There will be plenty to do along the way," Papa said. "A tutor will be traveling with the wagon train, and you children will have lessons along the way."

"Lessons?" Lucy and Lottie hollered out from inside the wagon. "Do we have to?"

"Yes, you have to," Mother replied.

Katie Sue didn't mind. It would make the time pass faster, after all.

"How far will we make it today, Papa?" Lottie called out to be heard above the rattling of the wagon. The youngster peeked up from the back of the wagon with a mischievous look on her face.

Right away, Lucy's face appeared too. She brushed a loose brown hair from her face, and grinned. For a minute there, she looked a bit like Papa. Then again, the twins had always favored Papa. Katie Sue favored Mama, in most ways, anyway. She had her blond hair and blue eyes, and folks always said she had her mom's smile. If only she could sing like Mama too.

"In fair weather we will manage about fifteen or twenty miles a day," Papa said. "If all goes well, we will reach the Mississippi River by the end of March."

"The end of March?" Katie Sue sighed as she put her hand over her eyes to shade them from the sun. There were still three weeks in March. Would it really take three weeks just to reach the Mississippi River? And how much longer after that? Why, the Mississippi River wasn't even halfway, was it?

She fixed her eyes on the road ahead, listening as Mama began to sing a happy little song about trusting in God. If there was anything Katie Sue loved, it was the sound of her mama's voice raised in song. All of a sudden, the team of mules stirred up a terrible amount of dust. Katie Sue pulled a hankie up over her eyes, but they were already stinging. She tried not to complain. After all, she did want to make Papa proud, but it was hard. To be honest, she just wanted to turn the wagon around and head right back home. Right away, the scripture about trust from Proverbs came to her mind. She whispered it in prayer and prayed for peace.

"I think I'd better get back in the wagon," she said at last, after feeling as if she'd swallowed several mouthfuls of dust.

Mama pulled the edges of her bonnet tight around her face and nodded. "Take good care of your little sisters. See that they don't get into trouble."

"Yes ma'am." She sighed, knowing her rapscallion sisters would probably want to jump about and play like boys, as always. Would they ever learn to be proper young ladies? Perhaps when they arrived in Texas, she would give them a few lessons.

Just then, something occurred to her. She turned back to whisper a question to her mother. "Mama, what will we do about bathing? I'm so dirty already!"

"Ah. When we come to a stop at a creek's edge, we will bathe and wash our hair in the creek."

"In the creek?" Katie Sue shook her head. "Truly?"

"Yes, along the trail the womenfolk bathe first, then the men. But don't fret, sweetheart. You will grow accustomed to the idea, with time."

Katie Sue scooted back into the wagon and felt herself tossed this way and that as the wagon jutted about. She was surprised to find the twins were sound asleep and soon joined them for a little nap.

After a couple of hours of riding, Mama woke them so that they could eat lunch together. As they ate, Papa's eyes lit with joy as he began to talk again about Texas, describing it as a wild and wonderful place—a place where they would farm the land, make new friends, and tell others about Jesus.

"Texas became a state in 1845. It has only been a state for about six years," he explained. "That's not very long, is it?"

"Six years! That's as old as me," Lottie piped up.

"You mean Texas is the same age as I am?" Lucy asked.

Papa chuckled. "Well, it may have only been a state for six years, but before that, it was the Republic of Texas after it won its independence from Mexico. It was its very own country before it actually became a state. Many in Texas are proud, to be sure."

"I've seen a picture of the Texas state flag," Katie Sue said. "It's quite lovely."

"Yes, it is," Papa remarked. "It's called the Lone Star Flag because of the large white star. And the colors of the flag represent something too. Red stands for bravery, white stands for purity, and blue stands for loyalty. Some people refer to Texas as the Lone Star State."

"Oh, I like that," Katie Sue said thinking about the large white star.

"We will settle in central Texas, in a place called Springfield, near Pole Cat Creek," Papa said.

"Pole Cat Creek?" Lucy's eyes grew large.

Papa nodded, then told them all about the adventures they would have once they arrived.

After lunch, the children decided to walk alongside the wagon for awhile. Papa brought the mules to a halt just long enough for Katie Sue to climb out. She used one of the big spoke wheels to step down. Lottie and Lucy jumped down, nearly falling in the process.

"Careful, girls!" Mama called out.

"I'm fine!" Lottie answered.

"Me too!" Lucy echoed.

Several of the girls Katie Sue had met the day before joined them, and before long, they were all walking and talking together. Why, if it hadn't been for the steep hilly road and the dust stirred by the wagons, Katie Sue might have forgotten she was traveling at all!

Peggy turned out to be a lot of fun, though she did like to talk a lot. She told a lot of funny stories and kept them all laughing.

"My mama is going to have a baby," she said with a smile, "but the baby isn't due till summer, so we should make it in plenty of time." She went on to talk about her father's plans to start a farm once they arrived in Texas.

"My Papa hopes to farm, as well," Katie Sue said with a nod, "but what he really wants to do is preach. He hopes to start a church once we arrive."

She peeked over at Josie, who had been awfully quiet. The youngster now wore a sturdy, plain traveling dress, and looked every bit like the other girls—not a bit snobbish, in fact.

"What will your father do in Texas, Josie?" Katie Sue asked.

Josie's face lit with a smile as she talked about her father's plans to work for the railroad once they arrived. "He is going to work for the BBB&C railroad. He says the railroad line will soon stretch all the way from Tennessee to Texas. Can you imagine?"

"Wouldn't that be wonderful?" Katie Sue could hardly believe it! Traveling by train would be much more enjoyable.

"It wouldn't take nearly as long as traveling by wagon," Josie explained, "and would be far more comfortable. Riding in these hills is so hard on the animals—and the people too!"

Katie Sue thought about what she had said. Perhaps, if the railroad track was laid from Tennessee to Texas, Matilda could come for a visit someday. Just the thought of it put a smile on her face.

The children walked and talked together until they reached a stretch of road filled with muddy holes, which Katie Sue did her best to avoid. She didn't want to get dirty. Still, the hem of her calico skirt was covered in brown stiff mud before long. "Oh, look at my dress," she said with a shrug.

Just about that time, Papa called out, "Into the wagon, children. We've a creek to cross."

Katie Sue said good-bye to the others and climbed back into the wagon, peeking out the back as the team of mules waded through the shallow water of a small creek. She opened her tiny locket and looked at Matilda's sweet face and had to wonder… Would Matilda have liked Peggy and Josie? Would she have walked alongside them, laughing and talking?

Katie Sue closed the locket and prayed long and hard for her friend. Her heart ached every time she thought about all she was missing back at home in Robertson County, Tennessee.

Still…

She gazed out of the back of the wagon at the others. Traveling to Texas *was* turning out to be a lot more fun than she had imagined, and she was meeting new people, just as Mama and Papa had said. Perhaps she could trust God to help her through this journey. She would trust in Him with all of her heart, just as the scripture said. "*Trust in the Lord with all of thine heart*," she whispered. Yes, that is just what she was going to do.

March 24, 1851

Dear Diary,

I can't believe we have been gone for two
weeks now. How I miss my best friend
in all the world. The first days on the
trail were long as we made our way up
and down through the mountains. My
beloved mountains are gone now, but
the countryside is very pretty as we travel
through rolling hills and cold streams.
The green of spring is starting to cover the
brown of winter and it reminds me that
every season brings something new and
wonderful. I can hardly wait to see the
spring flowers!

Sincerely,

Katie Sue

———⇒➤●◄⇐———

Katie Sue found herself caught up in the wonder of the moment, going round and round with the others, singing all the while.

———⇒➤●◄⇐———

SETTING UP CAMP

*T*HE NEXT WEEK ALONG THE TRAIL PASSED by quickly, although they were not without their troubles. Katie Sue heard Mr. McClintock tell Papa that one of the scouts had been badly injured when his horse galloped under a tree. The poor man was thrown off his horse and several bones were broken.

Katie Sue gave a little shiver as she thought about it. Thankfully, no one in her family was any worse for the wear. Except for a few blisters on their feet, the trip had been fairly smooth for the Herod family so far.

In the mornings, as the women packed up the wagons and the men readied the animals for the day's journey, the children would meet with Miss Grace, the tutor, to receive their daily school lessons. Katie Sue didn't mind the lessons at all. They were a nice distraction from the weariness of the trip. But several of the little boys and girls complained a lot, especially the twins. Katie Sue did her best to make them mind their manners, particularly in front of their tutor, Miss Grace. After they received their lessons, they would head back to their family wagons and complete their lessons along the trail.

With the exception of a light storm as the travelers made their way toward Memphis, the wagon train moved at a good speed. The Herod family, along with all of the others, arrived at the edge of the Mississippi River late on a Friday afternoon, just as March turned into April. A few springtime flowers greeted them as the wagons rolled along the steep bluffs overlooking the Mississippi River.

As usual, the wagons circled and set up camp for the night. Katie Sue had wondered why they would form a big circle with their wagons. "It's for protection," her papa explained. "If an enemy were to attack, we could defend ourselves better in this circle that serves as a fort."

As the sun dipped into the western sky, it cast orange shadows over the campsite. The menfolk scurried about, unyoking the mules and oxen, and feeding them corn, oats, and grain. Then they led the weary animals down to the river's edge to drink.

The children worked hard, milking cows, gathering firewood, and fetching water from the river. The twins always helped their papa, because they loved spending time with the animals. Katie Sue helped Mama shake out the quilts and hang them outside to air out.

The women worked together to build a campfire. Before long, a huge kettle of beans bubbled merrily above it. Katie Sue could hardly wait to eat a steaming bowl of savory beans. It seemed like they'd had dried venison and cold biscuits for days.

Not that she had minded, really. To her surprise, the trip had turned out to be great fun.

She looked about with a smile on her face. To think that only three short weeks ago she didn't know any of these people, and now they all felt like family to her. Peggy and her parents were wonderful friends now. And Josie…

Katie Sue smiled, thinking about Josie. She had turned out to be the best friend of all. The two girls had so much in common, they could scarcely stop talking. Day in and day out, they chattered like old friends.

She turned in the direction of the women, smiling as she saw her mother working alongside Josie's mother, roasting a large slab of pork that had been placed on the spit. Just the thought of ham and beans made Katie Sue's mouth water.

"Mama!" Katie Sue waved as she approached.

"Well, hello." Mama looked up with a smile. "Ready to bid farewell to Tennessee?"

Katie Sue drew in a deep breath. She couldn't believe this might be her last night in Tennessee—perhaps forever. Would she ever see Matilda again? A lump grew up in her throat, and she reached to touch her locket. As much as she loved her new friends, she would never, ever forget her best friend in the world. And as soon as she could, she would mail the letters she'd written along the way.

"Would you like to help stir up a batch of cornbread?" Mama asked. "I've got to keep an eye on the ham and tend to the coffee for the men."

"Yes ma'am." Katie Sue went to work at once, helping prepare the food.

Before long, everyone in the campsite had gathered around. Lanterns hung all about, flickering bits of light against the night sky. The whole place felt cozy and homelike.

A loud voice rang out across the crowd as the wagon boss approached. "I'm hungrier than an old, wild bear!" Mr. McClintock said, and then gave a ferocious growl.

The children all laughed. Well, all but one shy little girl named Maggie, who hid behind her mother's skirt.

Katie Sue had grown used to Mr. McClintock and his funny ways. She wasn't keen on his chewing tobacco or the way he spit the juice from it into a can. But his stories were funny, and his tanned, leathery face made for plenty of stories among the children. Some said he was a bank robber—on the run from the law. Others guessed him to be a pirate. Katie Sue had decided he was just a man who loved to travel—an adventurer, as Papa would say.

Speaking of Papa, he now stood to lead the group in prayer, as he did most every night when they stopped. In fact, some in the wagon train had taken to calling him "Preacher." Katie Sue loved the sound of his deep voice as he prayed, and could see what a fine preacher he would make.

There was only one sound Katie Sue loved more—her mother's voice raised in song. Why, Mama had the prettiest singing voice in all of Tennessee—probably in all of the country! Oh, how she wished she could sing like that! What good did it do to look like Mama if she couldn't sing like her?

After the prayer, the meal began and so did the laughter and the conversations.

All around, the smell of roasted meat and beans with molasses lingered in the air. Katie Sue loved that smell. After filling her metal plate with food, she found a place to sit near the chuck wagon on one of the empty water barrels.

Just two days ago, she and the other children had finally taken a peek inside the chuck wagon—at Mr. McClintock's invitation, of course. They'd found it to contain a host of drawers that held everything one would need for cooking—matches, food, and many utensils. There was even a space for large pots and pans, and even Dutch ovens.

"A rolling kitchen!" Mr. McClintock had said with a wink.

Indeed, it was.

Katie Sue had also enjoyed meeting the four mules that pulled the wagon: "Matthew, Mark, Luke, and John," Mr. McClintock had called them. "Good Bible names."

Even Papa had laughed at that one.

Of course, the mules were resting down by the water's edge now. They were plenty weary after three weeks of hauling the big wagon, no doubt. And there was plenty of work ahead for them, poor things. Once they crossed the Mississippi tomorrow, they'd have a long trek across Arkansas, like all the rest of the animals.

Katie Sue thought about Papa's mules for a minute as she nibbled on her food. They all seemed to be faring well, though he said their shoes would have to be replaced again before long. Thank goodness Papa knew how to shoe horses. Of course, there was a blacksmith in the wagon train, but Papa preferred to take care of his own animals.

Papa's voice interrupted Katie Sue's thoughts. "What are you thinking about, Duchess?" he asked.

"Oh, just thinking." She looked up at him with a smile as he settled down on the ground next to her.

"Thinking about what song you're going to ask Mama to sing tonight?" he asked with a playful look in his eye.

"Oh, Papa! Do you think she will?"

He nodded. "I hear tell there will be storytelling and a bit of singing. I'm sure she can be persuaded—if the right person asks, that is." He gave her a wink.

"I'll ask," she agreed, "but you must promise to play your fiddle. Will you?"

"I will," he nodded, "though it will have to be fetched from the memory trunk."

"Oh, yes sir! As soon as I'm finished with supper, I'll be glad to get it!" Katie Sue smiled as she thought about what the rest of the night would be like. How wonderful that her new friends would finally get to hear Papa play his fiddle and Mama sing. Why, she sang like a bird!

After she finished eating, Katie Sue slipped off to the wagon to fetch Papa's fiddle from the memory trunk. She carefully unlocked the lid of the large black trunk and gazed inside at all of the family's belongings. To think, this trunk had traveled all the way from Wales! Surely the journey from Tennessee to Texas didn't seem so far, compared to that!

Moments later, Katie Sue returned to find Papa chatting with Mr. McClintock. She handed her father the fiddle with a grin.

"Oh, are you going to entertain us with some music, Mr. Herod?" Mr. McClintock asked with a gleam in his eye. "I think that would be grand!"

"I would love to."

Papa began to tune his fiddle, and as soon as he did, everyone gathered around. One of the men pulled out a harmonica, and another reached for an accordion. Katie Sue could sense the excitement in the air. Why, there was something about music that always drew a crowd even out here under the open sky with stars twinkling above.

Before long, the strings on Papa's fiddle seemed to come alive. The other instruments joined in, and a melody poured forth. Folks began to sing the familiar song. Katie Sue joined in, tapping her foot and clapping her hands as she sang:

"Lost my partner, What'll I do?
Lost my partner, What'll I do?
Lost my partner, What'll I do?
Skip to my Lou, my darlin'."

The children began to skip around in circles as the song continued. Katie Sue found herself caught up in the wonder of the moment, going round and round with the others, singing all the while.

"Skip, skip, skip to my Lou,
Skip, skip, skip to my Lou,
Skip, skip, skip to my Lou,
Skip to my Lou, my darlin'.

"Off to Texas, two by two,
Off to Texas, two by two,
Off to Texas, two by two,
Skip to my Lou, my darlin'."

Exhausted after such a long dance, Katie Sue plopped down on the ground next to Josie, giggling merrily. Papa changed songs, and the familiar melody to "Turkey in the Straw" rang out. Several of the adults clapped their hands, and Mr. McClintock rose and sang out the verse in a booming voice:

"As I was a-gwine down the road,
With a tired team and a heavy load,
I crack'd my whip and the leader sprung,
I says day-day to the wagon tongue.
Turkey in the straw, turkey in the hay,
Roll 'em up and twist 'em up a high tuckahaw
And twist 'em up a tune called Turkey in the Straw."

As Papa played the fiddle merrily to accompany Mr. McClintock, Lottie and Lucy jumped up and began to dance a little jig. Katie Sue couldn't help but giggle as she watched her little sisters. They could be such show-offs at times.

The song ended at last, and Mr. McClintock took a bow. He gestured for the twins to do the same, and the little girls bowed low, grinning from ear to ear as folks applauded.

Finally, the moment came. Katie Sue approached Mama and asked if she would sing.

"Oh, I couldn't!" Mama looked embarrassed, but smiled anyway.

"You must, Mama. I haven't heard you sing in weeks and I miss it so! Besides…," Katie Sue gave her a little pout, "this is our last night in Tennessee, and I want to remember you singing here."

"Well, if you put it like that." Mama chuckled. "What song would you like to hear?"

"The one I love so much," Katie Sue said with a smile. "'Simple Gifts.'"

Mama nodded, and then began to sing the familiar song in a clear and beautiful voice. The words were so soothing, Katie Sue found her eyes growing heavy. Something about her mother's voice raised in song just made her happy and peaceful. All those words about trusting God just seemed to make more sense when Mama was singing.

> "'Tis the gift to be simple,
> 'Tis the gift to be free,
> 'Tis the gift to come down where we ought to be,
> And when we find ourselves in the place just right,
> It will be in the valley of love and delight.

"When true simplicity is gained,
To bow and to bend, we will not be ashamed
To turn, turn, will be our delight,
'Til by turning, turning, we come round right."

After her mother finished the beautiful song, everyone clapped and proclaimed she had the best singing voice they had ever heard. Katie Sue couldn't help but agree. Mama's cheeks turned pink, and she thanked them with a curtsy.

After that, a few of the men who traveled with the wagon boss began to tell what Papa called tall tales. Some of their stories were fanciful, but some—like the one about the Indians in Arkansas and Texas—frightened Katie Sue. The womenfolk finally put a stop to the stories, proclaiming bedtime had arrived.

Katie Sue reluctantly said goodnight to her friends and headed back to Herod House to sleep. As she settled in for the night, the words to "Skip to My Lou" seemed to echo in her ears:

Off to Texas, two by two,
Off to Texas, two by two,
Off to Texas, two by two,
Skip to my Lou, my darlin'.

Katie Sue dozed off at last, sad to be leaving her home in Tennessee, but fully trusting the Lord to see them through—all the way to Texas.

———⇒➤●⇐———

*She leaned over the rail of the boat
and stared down into the deep
waters of the mighty Mississippi.*

———⇒➤●⇐———

CROSSING OVER THE MISSISSIPPI

SATURDAY MORNING DAWNED BRIGHT AND clear. Katie Sue peeked her head out of the wagon to find many of the others already awake and working hard.

"I must've overslept," she whispered. Of course, she had stayed up later than usual last night, singing and dancing with her new friends. Perhaps she needed the extra sleep.

She yawned and leaned over to tap her little sisters on the arm. "Wake up, sleepyheads," she said with a giggle. "We're about to cross the river."

Lucy sat up right away and rubbed her eyes. "Really?"

"Really and truly?" Lottie echoed.

"Uh-huh." Katie Sue nodded and then stretched her arms. "We'll be in Arkansas before long." She pointed out to the campfire where her mother tended the coffee.

"Mama and Papa are already up working. We'd better join them."

Minutes later, she and her little sisters climbed out of the wagon, all dressed for the day's adventures. They approached the water barrel, where they splashed cold water onto their faces to freshen up.

"Mississippi River water," Lottie said with a smile.

Lucy took a little sip. "Tastes good!"

"Explorers for centuries have quenched their thirst with water from the Mississippi." Papa's voice rang out from behind them, startling them both.

"Good morning, Papa!" Katie Sue reached to give him a hug. "We're crossing over today!" She pointed off in the distance to the wide, beautiful river. She was excited about crossing over into Arkansas, but a little nervous about how they would get across such a large, flowing river.

"Indeed, we are crossing over, Duchess. Indeed we are," her father said. "I've already paid the ferry driver three whole dollars to carry us to the other side."

"Th…three d…dollars?" Katie Sue could scarcely get the words out, she was so amazed. Why, three dollars was a tremendous amount of money. Did it really cost that much to cross a river?

"This is a very special river," Papa continued, "filled with adventurous stories from days gone by."

"Tell us, please!" Lucy pleaded.

Papa's eyes lit up as he told of the many steamboats that traveled up and down the Mississippi River. "They are large, beautiful boats," he explained, "with huge paddle wheels powered by steam. The passengers aboard eat, sleep, and visit as they journey along. There is plenty of entertainment aboard for everyone—and a good time to be had by all."

Traveling by ship sounded a lot more fun than by wagon, Katie Sue had to admit.

"Will we see one today?" Lottie asked, her eyes growing large with excitement.

"Perhaps," Papa said with a twinkle in his eye. "Steamships travel south on the Mississippi River all the time carrying passengers all the way from the Ohio River to New Orleans!"

Katie Sue wasn't sure where the Ohio River was, and she surely didn't know where New Orleans was, but she didn't interrupt Papa's story to ask. She could see for herself that the Mississippi River was the widest and longest river she had ever seen. And from what Papa was saying, many a passenger traveled down it.

"If you got on a boat and traveled south," Papa explained, "you would float all the way down to the salty waters of the Gulf of Mexico. Of course, the Gulf is a far cry from here."

"Are *we* going south, Papa?" Lucy clapped her hands in glee.

"No, Lucy," Papa said, "not on this trip anyway. We are headed west." His eyes took on a dreamy look, as they often did when he talked about their new home. "We're setting out across the open land of Arkansas—all the way to Texas."

"Will we be there soon?" Lottie asked with a groan. "I'm tired of traveling."

"Oh my, no," Mama said, as she appeared with a plate of biscuits in her hand. "We are still weeks away."

Lottie pouted and turned her attentions back to the river once again.

"Yes, we've quite a ways to go yet," Papa said, as he patted Lottie on the back, "but what adventures we are having!" He looked back out at the waters once more. "There will be other rivers to cross along the way, but none as famous as the mighty Mississippi."

Mama held out the plate of biscuits with a happy look on her face. "Eat your fill," she said. "It might be several hours before we can eat again."

Katie Sue nibbled away at a biscuit and jam, but her mind was on other things. She could hardly wait to board the ferry—to cross the wide river called the Mississippi.

After they finished eating, the Herod family traveled along with others in the wagon train, slowly approaching the river's edge. There, they found a ferryboat—a keelboat, Papa called it.

"Look, Papa!" Lucy pointed at the mule-drawn tread-mill that operated the ferry.

"Yes, that is how the boat is pulled across," Papa explained. "Very clever, isn't it?"

"Very!" Katie Sue had to agree. In fact, she didn't know when she'd ever seen anything like it.

One by one the wagons were loaded on the ferry. The Herods waited for their turn. All the while, Katie Sue looked out over the beautiful Mississippi River, thinking of the stories Papa had told. She wished a steamboat would pass by so that she could see the huge paddle wheel and see the travelers onboard. Instead, all she saw was the long, flat ferryboat, crossing back and forth, carrying one wagon at a time.

Finally the awaited time arrived. A couple of men helped Papa unhitch the team from the wagon. Then, they all rolled the wagon onto the boat by hand. The mules were led aboard, and then the family entered. Katie Sue was so excited she could hardly contain herself. She leaned over the rail of the boat and stared down into the deep waters of the mighty Mississippi.

Mama held tight to Lottie and Lucy's hands as she gazed at the river. "It is lovely, isn't it!" she said with a dreamy sound in her voice. "I don't think I've ever seen anything more majestic. Have you?"

Katie Sue shook her head. "No ma'am." She reached with her fingertips to touch her little locket, thinking about Matilda. Her best friend would love the Mississippi River. Katie Sue felt sure of it.

"It must be the biggest river in the whole world!" Lottie declared.

"Sure looks like it!" Katie Sue agreed.

Just then, the boat gave a little jolt as it began to move from the shore. Katie Sue stumbled and almost lost her footing. Her hand, which had been clutching the locket, suddenly slipped, and she felt the chain break and slip through her fingers.

"Oh no! Oh no!"

At the very moment the locket began to fall, Papa appeared at her side. He managed to reach out and grab the locket and chain as they almost went over the edge of the boat into the water below. He clutched them in the palm of his hand, and Katie Sue began to cry.

"Oh, Papa! I thought I'd lost the locket forever. What would I have done?"

He drew her into a warm embrace. "Don't worry, Duchess. It's all right. Your locket is safe and secure." He held it up for a closer look. "The chain is broken, but never you mind about that. Once we settle in at the campsite tonight, I'll take a look at it. I feel sure I can fix it." He put it into his pocket and gave her a wink.

Katie Sue dried her eyes and nodded. "Thank you, Papa," she whispered. As always, he could make everything all right again.

She turned her attentions back to the ferry, not wanting to miss a thing. She closed her eyes and dreamed of traveling down the Mississippi River in a steamboat. Why, she could almost picture herself aboard one now! She would be dressed in the latest, beautiful fashions for such a grand journey.

It seemed only a few minutes had passed before the ferry arrived at the shoreline on the other side of the river.

"Welcome to Arkansas!" someone hollered out.

Katie Sue and the twins all smiled. "We're in another state." Even as Katie Sue spoke the words aloud, she realized the truth… she had *never* been in another state before—only Tennessee. Would Arkansas look different or feel different?

As the men worked together to get the wagons and animals off of the keelboat, Katie Sue was distracted by a loud sound, unlike anything she had ever heard before.

"Sister, look!" Lucy tugged on her sleeve, and she turned back to look at the river once again.

"Oh my!" She clamped a hand over her mouth, hardly believing what she was seeing. "Is it really…?"

Just as Papa had described it, a large steamboat approached from upriver. The huge paddle stirred the waters, causing them to churn. Before long, the keelboat was tipping back and forth from the waves, but that didn't alarm Katie Sue. No, she was far too excited, staring at the large white steamboat.

She waved at the passengers, and many waved back, hollering out hellos to the crowd on the ferry.

"Oh, Mama!" Katie Sue looked up at her mother with tears in her eyes. "This is the best day of my life. We have had a real adventure, unlike any other!"

"That we have, sweetheart," Mama said with a smile, "but just you wait. As wonderful as today has been, there are many more wonderful adventures ahead."

Katie Sue turned back for one last look at the steamboat as it moved on down the river. Yes, there might be adventures ahead. But for now, she was perfectly content with the one she was living—right here, right now.

———❖———

"This has been a hard journey,
but it'll be worth it in the end.
When we get to Texas…"

———❖———

Nine

ADVENTURES ALONG THE WAY

*T*HE FIRST TWO DAYS AFTER CROSSING the Mississippi went smoothly. Papa fixed Katie Sue's locket, and it was as good as new. She wrote about it in her diary. In fact, Katie Sue wrote in her diary almost every evening as the wagon train set up camp, putting all of her memories down on paper so that she would never, ever forget.

She wrote about the lovely springtime flowers she saw along the way, and the birds that whistled in the trees. She wrote about what it felt like to bounce up and down in the wagon. She wrote about how the land had grown flat after they crossed the Mississippi River. Papa had called it the lowlands and she certainly new why. She wrote about the different crops she saw as the wagon rolled along. And she wrote about the new friends she had made on the trail. She also wrote a wonderful letter to Matilda, telling her all about the ferry ride and the big white steamboat with its huge paddles.

Still, in spite of all of her adventures, Katie Sue grew a little weary with traveling. Sitting in the wagon for long periods of time was tiresome, but so was walking. By now, her backside ached, and so did her feet. The bottoms of her toes were more blistered than ever, and so were the backs of her heels where her shoes had rubbed against them. Papa's hands were raw from clutching the reins, and Mama's ankles were swollen, but they never seemed to complain.

Oh, if only the twins could be more like them! They had taken to whining much of the time, something that annoyed Katie Sue and Mama greatly, though—as proper ladies—they always tried to make the best of things.

On the third day into Arkansas, the weather took a turn for the worse. Papa led the team of mules, as always, though they seemed a bit skittish due to the thunder. Mama and the children huddled in the wagon, preparing for the storm. Overhead, the thunder rumbled, and every now and again a flash of lightning lit up the sky. Katie Sue couldn't help but worry. She'd overheard Mr. McClintock talking about lightening once. He'd said if it struck a wagon, the wagon might catch on fire! Right away, she began to pray silently that such a thing would never happen to them!

Mama tried to keep the children distracted by telling funny stories, but the wagon vibrated every time the thunder crashed overhead, which scared the twins. They buried their heads underneath a quilt and peeked out only now and again.

Katie Sue was frightened too, though she wouldn't have admitted it. She shivered as she crawled up to the front of the wagon and peeked outside.

"Looks like a spring storm," Papa called out. "Might not be pretty."

"Will we keep going even if it gets bad?" Katie Sue asked her father.

Papa did his best to control the mules before answering. After getting them calmed down, he turned back to look into the wagon at Katie Sue.

"We need to find a safe place to stop," he hollered out in order to be heard above a crash of thunder. "I believe there is a clearing up ahead. We will likely stop there until the storm passes. Looks like it'll be a doozy." He shook his head and spoke in a very serious voice, "A storm will likely bring in mosquitoes, and mosquitoes carry all sorts of disease."

Katie Sue tried not to worry, but the look on Papa's face didn't make her feel much better about things.

Within minutes the rain started. The oiled canvas on top of the wagon bows overhead kept most of the water out—at first. After awhile, tiny drops of water began to leak through. Mama pulled out a large cooking pot to catch the water. The twins, no longer afraid, seemed to find the whole thing entertaining.

"We're traveling in Noah's ark, Mama!" Lucy shouted. She pointed at the rain as it poured down.

"Before long we will be floating!" Lottie added.

"I surely hope not!" Katie Sue said.

"It looks like I'll have to fetch my needle and thread when the rain stops," Mama said as she looked up at the canvas. "I'll have to mend this wagon cover as soon as possible, or we will all be soaked before long!"

The wagon jutted up and down, up and down, as the rain created muddy holes in the road. More than once, Katie Sue bumped her head on the side of the wagon as it jolted this way and that. She hung on for a time but finally decided to ask Papa another question.

She crawled to the front of the wagon once again, amazed to find Papa, now soaking wet, still guiding the team of mules. "How much longer till we get to stop?" she asked.

Just then, the wagon jolted, and the mules let out a loud bray. The whole wagon tilted to the left, and Katie Sue lost her balance, nearly taking a tumble.

"We've broken a wheel, so it looks like we will have no choice but to stop now!" Papa shouted. He managed to get the mules stopped and settled down. He jumped down from his seat to tend to the wheel.

After a few minutes of waiting, Mama leaned out of the wagon. "James, may I help you?" she asked.

"No, Hannah, stay in the wagon with the children until the bad weather clears," he instructed. "Mr. McClintock has stopped the whole wagon train and has come back on horseback to assist me. Once the rain stops, we will have to unload the wagon so I can change the broken wheel."

Fortunately, the rainstorm passed quickly, and the Herod children were finally able to climb out of the wagon. Then the real work began. Everyone helped to unpack the loaded-down wagon with as much care as possible. The mud from the recent rainstorm didn't help matters much but everyone tried to be cheerful in the process. Finally, the wagon was completely empty. Papa and Mr. McClintock worked to brace up the side of the wagon and then removed the broken wheel. All the while, Papa talked to the children.

"This wooden center piece is called the hub," he explained, "and these small wooden rods that fasten the tire to the hub are called spokes."

"There are lots of spokes!" Lottie observed.

Papa nodded. "Anywhere from ten to twenty on each wheel." His eyes lit and Katie Sue knew a story was about to follow. "My father used to say the different spokes were all like the different Christian churches." He pointed to one spoke as he explained. "Imagine that one is Baptist." He pointed to another. "And that one is Methodist."

He chuckled as he pointed to yet another. "That one is Catholic, and so on and so forth!"

Katie Sue smiled as she thought about it. Why, just yesterday, she and Peggy had talked about the different churches they attended. Turned out, most of the people on the wagon train were from different kinds of Christian churches, but they all seemed to love the Lord just the same!

"Now you see," Papa explained, "that all of the spokes meet in the middle, at the hub."

"The hub is like heaven, then!" Katie Sue said, understanding Papa's story.

"Indeed," her father nodded, "and you are a very smart girl to figure that out!"

Katie Sue beamed from ear to ear. "Thank you."

Mr. McClintock and Papa finished replacing the wheel and then worked together to reload the wagon. Everyone pitched in to help and before long the wagon was reloaded with everything in its place.

"Now, would you help me with something, Duchess?" Papa asked.

"Certainly."

"I need you to get some feed for the mules from the trough on the back of the wagon," he explained. "The mules appear to be hungry."

"Yes sir." Katie Sue let out a sigh. Feeding the mules was a messy job—one she didn't care for. But after the rainstorm and unloading and then reloading the wagon, it didn't matter much. She was already quite a mess. She went around to the back of the wagon to the small wooden box that held the grain for the animals. She scooped it up and poured it into the mules' nose-bags and carried it around to the front of the wagon. Along the way, she carefully picked her way through the mud, trying her best not to totally ruin her dress. There, she stroked the neck of each mule as it ate. She listened quietly as Papa and Mr. McClintock talked.

"I'm concerned about two of my six mules," Papa said. "They've been reshod but still appear to be limping a bit. I think the journey has exhausted them, and I would hate to see anything happen to them." He shook his head and whispered, "I hear Mr. Tompkins had to shoot one of his mules."

"Broken leg," McClintock said. "There was nothing else to be done."

Katie Sue shivered as she thought about that. She continued to stroke one of the mules—a large brown one—and whispered in his ear: "We will never let that happen to you!"

"Many of the livestock are struggling," McClintock continued. "Some have been pulling loads far too heavy. To be honest, the wear and tear on the animals is causing a few of the wagons to slow down the whole group, and that's not a good thing for the rest of us."

"Yes," Papa agreed. "I noticed several families lightening their loads—leaving furniture and other expensive furnishings behind on the trail."

"The same thing happens on every trip," Mr. McClintock said with a shrug. "Folks overpack, forgetting their animals will have to pull such a heavy load."

"And the warm weather surely isn't helping the situation any," Papa added. "The spring temperatures seem to be much warmer west of the Mississippi."

"I'll say! Some of the oxen have grown restless in the heat, and that's a real problem," Mr. McClintock said. "Oxen have a tendency to stampede when restless."

Katie Sue's eyes grew large, but she didn't say anything. She had never seen a stampede before, and hoped she never would!

"Likely we will stop and set up camp for a few days along the banks of the Arkansas River," Mr. McClintock continued. "The town of Little Rock will be a fine place to replenish our supplies and give our livestock a rest."

Papa nodded. "Till then, we will just have to pray the animals and the wagon wheels make it in one piece."

"That we will," Mr. McClintock agreed.

Papa shook his head. "This has been a hard journey, but it'll be worth it in the end. When we get to Texas..." His eyes lit up with joy as he spoke. "When we get to Texas, there will be land in abundance and all the river water our animals could ever ask for."

He continued on with great zeal. Katie Sue finished feeding the animals and then joined Mama and the twins inside the wagon as they headed out on their way once more.

"I heard Mr. McClintock tell Papa we will stay on in Little Rock a few days to give the animals a rest," Katie Sue said.

Mama sighed. "I could use the rest, myself. I'm mighty tired. And I hear-tell Peggy's mama isn't feeling well at all. This journey has been very difficult on her."

Katie Sue thought about her friend's mother for a minute. Why, Mrs. Tompkins' baby wasn't due until later in the summer. Hopefully, they would make it to Texas before the little one arrived.

"How long till we get to Little Rock?" Lucy's voice took on a whining tone once again as she asked the question.

"Another week or so, little one," Mama said. "Just be patient."

"I don't know how to be patient," she grumbled. "How do I do that?"

Mama let out a laugh—the first one Katie Sue had heard all day. "Patience is all about waiting, and waiting is all about trusting."

Lucy let out a huff and leaned against the side of the wagon. "I'm mighty tired of waiting."

Katie Sue didn't say anything, but she was a little tired of waiting too. Hopefully they would arrive in Little Rock soon. Once there, she and her friends could spend a few days playing together and getting the rest they needed before heading out onto the trail once more.

Katie Sue swatted at a couple of pesky mosquitoes, then leaned back against Mama's quilt and settled down for an afternoon nap. Perhaps tomorrow would be a better day.

———⟫●⟪———

She prayed all night long, hardly
getting a wink of sleep.

———⟫●⟪———

TROUBLE FOR THE TRAVELERS

HE NEXT WEEK, AS SPRINGTIME FLOWERS were in full bloom, the wagon train pulled into the bustling town of Little Rock and set up camp. Katie Sue was happy to be in a new place, and especially happy to rest a few days alongside the banks of the Arkansas River. However, they'd no sooner settled in than the trouble started. Lottie began to complain of itching all over, and couldn't seem to stop scratching. Soon thereafter, Lucy started itching, as well.

"They both feel a bit feverish," Mama said, as she laid her palm on each forehead. "And look at this terrible rash! I do hope they haven't come down with something."

"Not likely they are really sick," Papa said. "I'd wager a guess they've come in contact with poison ivy."

"I will bathe them from head to toe," Mama said.

"I don't want a bath!" Lucy argued.

"Hush now, Daughter," Mama said. "A bath will cleanse the sores. Afterwards, I'll mix up a little oatmeal paste and spread it around on the itchy spots."

With Katie Sue's help, Mama took water from one of the wooden barrels and heated it in a kettle over the open fire so that two squirming little girls could be bathed. Once they were clean, Mama mixed up an oatmeal paste and spread it on all of the itchy spots. The girls never once stopped complaining as she worked to make them feel better.

Finally, Mama turned her attention to Katie Sue. "How are you feeling? I do hope you're not taking ill."

"I feel fine, Mama," Katie Sue said with a shrug.

"We will pray," Papa said, "and we will trust God. He will take care of us all. I know He will, because He always has. God is trustworthy."

Katie Sue nodded her head in agreement. She had been learning to trust God for everything, and she felt a peace in her heart.

Papa began to pray in his rich, loving voice. Katie Sue loved to hear her Papa's prayers almost as much as she loved to hear Mama sing. She began to look forward to him starting a church once they arrived in Texas. Surely then she would get to hear him pray a lot.

After Lottie and Lucy drifted off to sleep, Katie Sue asked if she could play with her friends.

"For a few minutes, I suppose," Mama said. "Then I will need your help with supper."

"Yes ma'am." Katie Sue climbed out of the wagon and stretched her legs. How wonderful it felt to be camped at last!

She looked around for Peggy, but couldn't find her out with the other children. She approached Josie with a smile on her face. "We'll be in Texas in another week!"

"Yes, I can't wait." Josie gave a little shrug. "I'm travel weary."

"Me too!"

"Did you hear about Peggy's mother?" Josie asked.

"No." Katie Sue's heart skipped a beat. "I do hope she hasn't had the baby yet!"

"No, not that." Josie lowered her voice as she explained. "My Papa says she has yellow fever. She's very sick."

"Yellow fever!" Katie Sue clamped a hand over her mouth. She could hardly believe it. Yellow fever was a very dangerous disease. "Are you sure?"

"Quite sure. Doc Madison says it's caused from the mosquitoes. He came by our wagon to warn us to keep our distance. I hear she's very ill. My Papa says there are three others in the camp sick with the fever, as well, including two of the children."

At the word "children" Katie Sue grew worried. "The twins are sick too," she whispered. "I do hope it's not…"

"Surely not," Josie said, patting her on the shoulder. "Let's hope not, anyway."

By nightfall, everyone in the camp had heard about Peggy's mother and the other sick folks. Mr. McClintock gathered everyone around the campfire for a conversation about the situation. Tonight, there would be no singing and dancing. No, the look on his face was quite serious.

"I'm sure you've all heard," he explained. "We've an outbreak of yellow fever in the camp. I was afraid of that, after the rains we faced a few days back. We know of at least four cases so far, and suspect a few more." The people began to murmur in fear, and he shushed them with these words: "In order to isolate the problem, we have quarantined the affected wagons."

"What are the symptoms?" one of the mothers asked. "What should we be watching for?" She clutched her little girl close with a worried look on her face.

"I'll let Doc Madison answer that," Mr. McClintock responded.

The doctor stood and faced the crowd. "The symptoms for yellow fever are similar to influenza—fever, muscle aches, headache, and so forth. In some cases, patients will have a red tongue or flushed face. I've even seen some reddening of the eyes."

As he spoke, Katie Sue thought about Lottie and Lucy. They didn't seem to have any of those symptoms, other than a slight fever, of course.

"Sadly," Doc Madison continued, "yellow fever often turns on the internal organs. I've seen cases where the heart was affected, or the liver." He paused and shook his head. "Yellow fever is a terrible disease, and everyone should avoid contact with those infected. That's why we have made the very difficult decision to leave the infected wagons behind when we set out on the final leg of our journey to Texas."

A gasp went up from the crowd. Many of the people turned to each other, murmuring among themselves. They simply didn't want to believe it could be true.

"Leave them behind?" Katie Sue looked at Mama in shock. Would they really leave Peggy and her family behind? And those poor sick children! Who would stay, to look after them? Doc Madison, perhaps? No, he would surely move on with the group. Others would need him along the way. She guessed they would be cared for by the doctor in Little Rock.

Mama nodded, and her face paled as she whispered, "Sadly, yes. Yellow fever is extremely contagious. Extremely."

Katie Sue didn't like the way Mama said "extremely" but didn't say anything. In her heart, she had to wonder about her little sisters. Did they have yellow fever too?

Would the Herod family have to stay behind when the wagon train left next Monday?

She prayed all night long, hardly getting a wink of sleep. By the end of her prayers, she knew she had to put the twins in God's hands and trust Him completely. Thankfully, by the next day, Lottie and Lucy felt much better. Their fever passed, though the itchy spots remained.

"See?" Papa asked with a smile. "Poison ivy, just as I said."

"Yippee!" Lottie celebrated with her arms raised in glee.

"You don't appear to be any worse for the wear." Papa smiled, and then prayed a prayer of thanksgiving. Katie Sue breathed a sigh of relief, knowing her little sisters were going to be just fine.

A few minutes later, Lucy slipped out of the wagon with a look of pure joy on her face.

"Did Mama say you could play?" Katie Sue asked.

The youngster nodded. "Yes, so long as I don't run about and get myself worked up," she explained. "I'm going to look for grasshoppers with my friends."

"A very tomboyish thing to do," Katie Sue said with a sigh. Would her sisters ever learn that they were little girls, not boys?

Katie Sue decided to join some of the other children near the campfire sight. As she drew near, she could tell at once that something terrible had happened from the look on Josie's face.

"What is it?" she asked.

"Peggy's mama," Josie whispered. "Doc Madison says she's probably not going to make it more than another day or so. She's taken a turn for the worse."

"W…what? Oh no!" Katie Sue sat on a nearby log and dropped her head into her palms. "That's terrible. Poor Peggy! And the baby. What will happen to the baby?"

Josie shook her head. "Mama says there's little hope for the baby. It's just awful, isn't it?"

"Yes." Katie Sue shook her head and did her best not to cry. Just then, she looked over at her little sisters who played nearby with their friends. She was grateful their symptoms had passed. Why, just the thought of losing them made her so sad, she could hardly bear it. Just as quickly, her heart broke for Peggy. How in the world would she manage to go on if she lost her mother?

By the next day, Katie Sue got the answer to her question. Sometime in the early morning hours, Peggy's mother passed away. Katie Sue could hear the shrill cries of the family, even from their wagon, and she cried along with them. She rocked back and forth, clutching her knees to her chest, sobbing all the while.

"It's n…not f…fair, Mama," she whispered. "It's not! What will Peggy do? And her Papa? What will her brothers and sisters do without their mother?" Her heart nearly broke just thinking about it.

Mama wiped a tear from her eye as she answered. "They will go on living, sweetheart. That's what you do when tragedy strikes—you go on. And somehow in the midst of it, you remember that God is for you, not against you. You keep on trusting Him, even when things are really, really hard."

"Trust Him… even now?" Katie Sue shook her head, completely confused. "It just doesn't make sense. God could have healed Peggy's mama if He wanted to. Couldn't He?"

"Yes." Mama gave her an understanding look. "But trusting God makes the most sense during times like this," Mama explained. "Remember that scripture you memorized back home in Tennessee?"

Katie Sue nodded but didn't say anything.

"*Trust in the Lord with all thine heart,*" Mama began, "*and lean not unto thine own understanding.*" She reached to take Katie Sue's hand in her own and gave it a squeeze.

Katie Sue wiped away her tears. "I remember," she whispered.

"During times like these, we cannot lean on our own understanding," Mama said as she brushed a loose hair from Katie Sue's face. "There are some things we will never figure out on our own. We just have to know that God is in control, and He is trustworthy."

Katie Sue did her best to fall back asleep. For once, she wished she could dream of Matilda. Wished she could dream of starting a church in Texas with Papa, or a school where she would meet new friends.

Instead, she could only think of poor, dear Peggy… and the more she thought about her, the harder she cried. She finally fell asleep though her dreams were unpleasant.

The very next morning, as the wagon train was about to set out on its way once more, Josie came by the Herod's wagon.

"May I ride with you for a spell?" she asked.

"Of course, dear," Katie Sue's mama said.

Josie climbed inside and settled into a comfortable spot next to Katie Sue. As the wagon jutted forward, Josie began to talk.

"It's so sad about Peggy's mama," she said with a sigh. "Don't you agree?"

"Truly, one of the saddest things I've heard," Katie Sue said.

"Can I ask you a question?" Josie looked up with a curious look in her eyes. "What do you think happens to people when they die?"

"They go to heaven," the twins spoke in unison.

"But…how do you know?" Josie asked. "I mean, do you really, really know that they do?"

"I've heard Papa preach about this a great many times," Katie Sue said. "He always says that in order for a person to go to heaven, they have to ask Jesus to come and live in their heart. They must ask for forgiveness for their sins."

Josie's eyes grew large. "I can't just get into heaven if I behave myself?"

Katie Sue shook her head. "No, going to heaven doesn't have anything to do with good deeds."

"Thank goodness!" the twins said in unison.

Katie Sue smiled as she continued on. "Though God *does* want us to live right and behave because it's the right thing to do. But going to heaven is all about accepting what Jesus Christ did on the cross."

"What did He do?" Josie looked at her curiously.

"He died for our sins." Katie Sue looked at her with great interest. "Do you mean you've never heard this story before?"

"No, never."

Katie Sue could hardly believe it. Why, she had heard this story dozens of times. "God sent his Son, Jesus, into the world," she explained, just as she'd heard Papa do, time and time again. "Even though He lived a sinless life, He died on a cross for us. He took our sins upon Himself. And when we accept Jesus—and ask Him for forgiveness—we are washed whiter than snow."

"Whiter than snow?"

"Yes, that means all the bad things we've ever done are washed away. They are forgiven. And we can begin again, with a clean slate!"

"H…how do I do that?" Josie asked. "Can you help me?"

Katie Sue took her by the hand. "Of course! We will pray together, and you can ask Jesus to come and live in your heart right now. He will, you know! Just as soon as you ask."

The girls bowed their heads and prayed. Even as the words poured forth, Katie Sue thought about Papa—how he wanted to go to Texas and lead others to the Lord. Why, if they hadn't been on this wagon train headed for Texas, she would never have met Josie. And if she'd never met Josie, she would have never had the chance to pray with her.

A smile crept across Katie Sue's lips. Suddenly, she understood. She knew why Papa wanted to share the Gospel with others. Leading someone to the Lord felt wonderful. In fact, it was the best feeling she'd had in a mighty long time.

April 20, 1851

Dear Diary,

We are only two days away from the Red
River. We will soon be leaving Arkansas.
The countryside always seems to be
changing here. When we first arrived,
the flat land seemed to stretch before
me forever. I could see for miles without
hardly a tree to hinder my view. But
as the wagon train neared Little Rock,
we reached the foothills of the Ouachita
Mountains. I instantly fell in love
with them, for they eased my homesick-
ness for my own Tennessee mountains.
After we left Little Rock, we came to a
place called Hot Springs, where hot spring
water bubbles in large pools out of the
ground. The Indians call it "Valley of the
Vapors." Mr. McClintock let us set up
camp there and bathe in the wonderful,

hot springs. It was like heaven after bathing in the cold creeks along the trail. Mama even surprised us with some candy she had bought at the mercantile in Little Rock. It was quite a treat. We have left the Ouachita Mountains now and are looking forward to the last leg of our journey. After we cross the Red River, we will finally be in Texas. I can hardly wait!

Sincerely,
Katie Sue

---

*"We're in the promised land now,
Herods! Welcome to Texas!"*

WELCOME TO TEXAS, KATIE SUE!

ATIE SUE GREW MORE EXCITED WITH each passing day. The wagon train arrived at the Texas border the third week in April. Despite the sadness everyone still felt, Katie Sue made up her mind to trust God with the rest of the journey. She looked forward to crossing over the Red River into a brand new state—a big, wonderful state where she would live in a new home with her family. What an adventure that would be!

Now, as she stared with wonder at the colorful river that separated Arkansas from Texas, she looked up at Papa with a smile. "It really *does* look red, just like Mr. McClintock said."

"It's the clay that gives it that color," Papa explained. "The water isn't really red at all."

"I see." She glanced across the wide expanse of the river then turned to look at her father again with a question on her mind. "Will we be ferried over?" she asked.

"Not this time," Papa told her. "This time we will find a spot where the river is shallow enough to wade through and we'll cross over on foot. The wagons are designed to float if they have to, so we should be fine. Afterwards, we will set up camp for a few days. Then, sadly, we will have to part ways with many of our friends."

That idea made Katie Sue very sad. She had already said good-bye to Peggy back in Little Rock. Here, at the border of Texas, she would have to say good-bye to Josie, as well. It seemed there had been a lot of good-byes in her life lately.

Katie Sue decided to make the best of things, not complaining, but looking forward to her new life. She repeated the scripture from Proverbs 3:5-6 over and over in her mind: "*Trust in the LORD with all thine heart; and lean not unto thine own understanding. In all thy ways acknowledge him, and he shall direct thy paths.*"

Just thinking about those words made her feel much better.

The next couple of hours were very adventurous as each of the wagons made the crossing at the narrowest point in the river. This proved to be one of the biggest adventures yet! Many of the animals were skittish about getting into the water, and several had to be prodded.

"Stay inside the wagon, children!" Mama called out. "And keep an eye on our belongings...that they don't jostle about. It's going to be a bumpy trip!"

"Yes ma'am," Katie Sue responded. She instructed the twins to sit still, and she went about the business of making sure the loose items in the wagon stayed put.

"Get along!" Katie Sue heard Papa holler out as their mules refused to cooperate. They finally stepped off into the water, and the wagon began to creep across the rocky river bottom.

Katie Sue prayed all the while that the current wouldn't grab hold of the wagon and drag it downstream. Her heart—which felt like a lump of lead—pounded in fear, and she clung to the side of the wagon with all her might. She kept telling herself to trust God and everything would be okay.

After what seemed like an eternity, they made it to the other side where they joined the others in a rousing cheer.

"I feel as if we've crossed the Jordan River!" Papa said, referring to the river mentioned in the Bible. "We're in the promised land now, Herods! Welcome to Texas!"

Afterwards, though it was still quite early in the afternoon, the wagon train set up camp in a large clearing just a few hundred yards west of the river near an Indian trading post. The men went to the trading post to purchase supplies while Mama and the other women gathered together all of the dirty clothes and quilts and headed to the water's edge to give them a good scrubbing.

As they approached the river, Katie Sue noticed Mama stop quite suddenly. "What's wrong, Mama?" she asked.

Her mother gestured to the edge of the river, where several women worked alongside one another washing clothes. The women had lovely tanned skin and shiny black braided hair. They wore colorful beaded deerskin blouses and woven skirts—unlike anything Katie Sue had ever seen before. Some leaned down at the water's edge, fetching water. Others worked hard, scrubbing their clothes against the rocks.

Katie Sue watched in wonder, then looked up at her mother with a question. "Who are they, Mama?" she asked.

"Indians." Her mother whispered the word, and a little shiver went down Katie Sue's spine. "Caddos, likely."

"Indians?" she whispered back. Why, Indians didn't look like this at all—not from the stories she'd been told, anyway. These women and children weren't at all frightening looking.

"What are Caddos?" Katie Sue asked her mother.

"The Caddos are an Indian tribe that live along the Red River and farm. They are how Texas got its name. The Caddo Indians called their tribes the 'Tejas' which means 'those who are friends.'"

"Oh. I never knew that," Katie Sue said looking at the group of dark-skinned people.

Several of the Indian mothers looked up as the women from the wagon train approached. Their eyes widened in fear, and a couple of them called out to their children in a language unfamiliar to Katie Sue. She watched in amazement as the children stared at them in terror.

"Are they scared of *us*, Mama?" she whispered.

"I'm not sure. Perhaps."

What an interesting thought! Why, no one had ever been scared of her before.

Mama and the others slowly and cautiously made their way down to the edge of the water to work alongside the women. Eventually, everyone seemed to overcome their fears, and they dove into their work with a vigor—all but the children, of course. They gazed at one another in curiosity. Katie Sue wished she could understand the language of the dark-haired youngsters. They seemed curious about her blond hair, pointing and whispering. She was a little scared at first but eventually grew used to being talked about. Oh, if only she could understand what they were saying!

The twins didn't seem to mind the language barrier. They went right up to one of the little girls about their same age and played with her long dark braid of hair. Why, in no time, they'd made several new friends. Many of the little Indian boys gathered around, and before long, they had a rousing game of marbles going. Katie

Sue helped her mother with the washing but kept a watchful eye on her sisters as they continued to play.

After playing marbles, several of the children took to splashing in a shallow pool of water at the river's edge.

"May I, Mother?" Katie Sue asked.

"Just be careful!"

Katie Sue unlaced her shoes and then pulled off her stockings so that she could run and play in the water. It was cool against her bare feet, and she ran about, playing with the others, enjoying every moment. Even Josie pulled off her shoes and splashed about.

"I can't believe what fun I'm having, doing tomboyish things," Katie Sue said with a laugh. "Why, back in Tennessee I would never have worn muddy skirts and pranced about in the river in bare feet!"

"Is that why your Papa calls you 'Duchess?'" Josie asked. "Because you're so. . ."

"Girlie?" Katie Sue giggled. "I suppose. One day when I told him I hated getting dirty like the twins, he called me his duchess, and the name just stuck."

She thought about it even as she spoke the words. These days, she didn't feel so much like a duchess. No, with each day that passed, she felt more like an adventurer, a pioneer.

After a few minutes of playing, one of the little Indian girls approached with a shy look on her face. After a minute or two of staring, she gently lifted her hand to touch Katie Sue's blond hair. Katie Sue didn't say a word but offered up a smile. The little girl then noticed Katie Sue's locket, and reached to touch it with her fingertip. Katie Sue opened it, revealing the pictures inside.

At once, the little girl began to speak quite loudly in her Indian tongue. She called for her friends, and within seconds, Katie Sue was surrounded by squealing little girls. What they were squealing about, she couldn't be sure.

One by one, they all stared at the photographs in her locket. One of the girls pointed at the picture of Katie Sue then looked up at her with a look of wonder, as if trying to figure out how she could be in two places at once.

"Oh, I see," Josie whispered, "they've never seen a photograph before! It must be very confusing!"

Though Katie Sue was happy to show off her locket, being surrounded by so many strangers was a little scary. More than once, she wondered if this was what Texas was always going to be like. Would she always feel like a stranger? Or would she get to know the people and get over her fears of being different?

She looked down once more at the photographs in the locket, smiling as her gaze fell on Matilda. How she wished her best friend could be here beside her! Matilda would make everything better. She closed the locket quite suddenly, determined not to think about things that would make her sad. No, this was a new day—no turning back. With a determined heart, she turned back to her work.

A short time later, the Indian women finished up their washing and headed off on their way. The children lingered for a moment but then tagged along behind their mothers. Katie Sue turned her attentions to her mother once again, helping drape several large, wet items of clothing to dry. Josie stood nearby, helping her mother as well. Before long, the two girls got to talking about the children they'd just met. Then their conversation took a turn.

"Our family is headed to Springfield," Katie Sue said. "That's southwest of here."

"Our family is going south," Josie said. "To Harrisburg—the place where Texas won her independence from Mexico at the Battle of San Jacinto. The railroad is going in, and before long, train tracks will be laid all the way from south Texas to the north! That's what my father says, anyway."

"Perhaps I can travel by train to see you someday!" Katie Sue suggested.

"That would be wonderful!"

Still, in spite of their joyful plans, Katie Sue knew the truth. After they parted ways, she would probably never see Josie again. And the very idea nearly broke her heart. "Why, Lord?" she whispered. "Why?" It seemed she was always having to say good-bye to those she loved.

With that question in her heart, she headed off to play with Josie. She tried not to think about the fact that it might be for the very last time.

---

*She decided right then and there
that Texas in the springtime was
every bit as pretty as Tennessee in
the fall, maybe even more so.*

A Brand New Life

KATIE SUE AND HER FAMILY PARTED ways with Josie and many of the others on the wagon train and began the long journey to central Texas—to the place Papa had called Springfield. A handful of other families traveled with them, but sadly, Josie's family was not one of them. Instead, they headed south—to Harrisburg.

"How long will it take to get to Springfield, Papa?" Lucy asked, as she sat alongside their father at the front of the wagon. "I'm tired of life on the trail. I want to live in a house again!"

"Me too!" Katie Sue agreed. She couldn't wait to see what kind of a home Papa would build for them when they arrived. Would it be a two-story one like their house in Tennessee? Would it have lovely maple trees they could climb?

"Hmm." Papa thought about it a moment before answering. "It's about 250 miles from here to our new home. We're traveling about 15 miles a day…on good days, when the weather cooperates. If we keep going at this rate, I'd say we'll be on our piece of land in less than 3 weeks."

"Three weeks?" Lucy groaned as the wagon bounced up and down. "Every week feels like a year!"

"Seems like we've been on the trail forever!" Lottie threw in.

"Well then…," Papa turned to them with a smile, "You should be very old women by now, not little girls!"

Lottie and Lucy chuckled, and then stopped their whining.

Katie Sue leaned back against the edge of the wagon, deep in thought. She couldn't stop thinking about Josie. She missed her friend terribly. She thought about something else too—how she'd almost missed out on a friendship with Josie in the first place.

You can't always tell about a person at first glance. Wasn't that what Mama always said? At first glance, Josie had seemed standoffish and a little stuck-up. But she wasn't that way at all! Why, she'd turned out to be kind-hearted and loving, and in many ways a better friend than any Katie Sue had ever known.

"Hmm." Her thoughts shifted again as she remembered the Indian women she'd seen at the river. At first glance, they'd seemed frightening. But after a little while, they'd proven to be quite friendly. Perhaps the same was true with them as with Josie. Had she judged them too quickly? Mama always said you shouldn't judge a person by outward appearances, and surely she was right! Had *that* been one of the many lessons God was trying to teach Katie Sue?

Perhaps this whole thing about trusting the Lord with all of her heart wasn't just what she'd thought. Maybe she could trust Him with the big things—like moving halfway across the country, *and* the smaller things—like bringing good friends into her life.

Her heart swelled with joy as she thought about all of the wonderful lessons she'd learned. Yes, the Lord was surely trustworthy, just as Papa had said.

The weeks seemed to fly by. Katie Sue loved traveling through the vast countryside of Texas. Gone were the mountains of Tennessee. In their place, were thick green piney forests filled with beautiful trees and flowers. After they had crossed through the piney forests, they came upon rolling hills with lakes and wide open fields filled with spring flowers. One day as they were traveling through the fields, Katie Sue saw some beautiful blue flowers off in the distance.

"What are those flowers, Mama?" she asked. "I don't think I've ever seen anything quite like them."

"Ah." Her mother stopped for a moment to stare at the pretty flowers. "I believe those are Texas bluebonnets.

Your papa has told me about them—said they were lovely, and they are!"

"Indeed." Katie Sue stared in wonder at the field, filled with bright blue flowers. Why, they were very nearly the same color as her eyes, she thought. And spread out over the field like that, they reminded her of one of Mama's quilts. They were simply beautiful.

She decided right then and there that Texas in the springtime was every bit as pretty as Tennessee in the fall, maybe even more so. Somehow, just looking at the flowers made her happy, and tonight she would write about it all in her diary.

The bluebonnet soon became everyone's favorite flower. Katie Sue loved to pick bouquets and hang them along the side of the wagon. They made her heart want to sing! And they made Mama's heart want to sing too. In fact, Mama made up a little song about the flowers, just to keep the children happy.

"I love the hills of Tennessee
With autumn leaves, and stately trees
But Texas flowers, they are the best
Better still, than all the rest.

"Oh, the little bluebonnets!
Oh, the little bluebonnets!
Oh, the little bluebonnets!
They cause the heart to sing!"

Katie Sue and the twins joined in, singing to their hearts' content. Something about singing with Mama got them so excited!

Besides singing, the Herod family kept busy in other ways—talking about all of the things they would do once they arrived on their property.

"We are quite blessed," Papa explained. "We own several hundred acres of land, so there will be plenty of room to build a home, care for livestock, and farm, if we like."

"Will we build a church?" Katie Sue asked.

"We will build a schoolhouse, and it will serve as a place of learning as well as a church," he explained.

The Herods turned their attention to talking about the house they would build and all of the furnishings that would go inside. Mama was especially happy to have so many of her belongings from the old house, but she looked forward to purchasing some new items too.

"I can't wait to sleep in a real feather bed again," Mama said with a sigh. "Though the wagon has certainly given us adequate shelter."

"I've enjoyed the nights we've slept outside under the stars," Papa commented. "And we will have a few more of those once we arrive in Springfield, for it will take several months to build the house."

His eyes lit up, and Katie Sue knew a story would follow. Papa just loved talking about how he would build their new home.

"Our land is in the post oak savannah," he explained, "so we will build a log house out of oak. The logs will be notched and fitted together at the corners, from trees we will cut down. To fill in the cracks, we will chink the walls with mortar."

"Will it be a two-story house, like our home in Tennessee?" Katie Sue asked.

"Indeed," Papa explained, "and I hope to build a lovely balcony upstairs." He gave her a little wink. "If you like that idea."

"Oh, I do!" She could hardly wait to sit out on the balcony and look out over their stretch of land.

"Tell them about the fireplace, James," Mama said.

"We will have a large stone fireplace," Papa said with a smile. "For cooking—and to keep the house warm in the wintertime." He went on to tell them more about the furnishings he would make, and with every word, Katie Sue grew more excited.

The days now passed quickly as the family's excitement grew. By the time they arrived in Springfield, she at once felt at home. The wagon came to a stop on a stretch of land like nothing else she had ever seen in all of her life. She looked about with a smile on her face.

"Oh, Papa! It's lovely!"

"It is," her mother agreed. "It certainly is."

"It's nothing like Tennessee," Katie Sue said to Papa. "I don't see mountains or steep hills at all, but those fields are beautiful!" She pointed off in the distance where high waving grass blew in the wind.

"That's sedge grass," Papa explained. "It grows thick and high as wheat! And off in the forest…" he gestured to a thicket of trees to their right, "you will find wildlife in abundance—buffalo, deer, antelope, jackrabbits, even armadillos. We won't lack for food, to be sure!"

"Armadillos?" Lottie asked. "What is an armadillo?"

Papa smiled. "The armadillo is an animal about the size of a cat."

"Can I play with them?" Lucy asked.

"Better not try!" Papa advised. "Their hard shells protect them from predators. Texas is filled with armadillos, so we will likely find many of them." He leaned down and whispered, "I hear-tell they are quite tasty!"

Katie Sue gave a little shiver. She couldn't imagine eating such a thing. Perhaps, with time, she would grow used to the idea!

"There are also rattlesnakes," Papa warned. "Better watch out for those. I hear they're everywhere in Texas."

"Snakes?" Katie Sue squeezed her eyes shut and tried not to think about it. Moments later she climbed out of the wagon and followed behind Mama and Papa as they walked their land. Together, they decided where they would build the house and the barn. On the edge of the property ran a beautiful, clear stream which Papa proclaimed to be full of fish. What fun they would have fishing along its banks.

As the day came to an end, Katie Sue thought about all of her many adventures along the trail. They had come so far—leaving a wonderful home in Tennessee. And yet…as she looked around this beautiful patch of land in Texas, she couldn't help but believe Papa had been right all along.

"We are supposed to be here," she whispered. "This is our home. Texas is our new home."

She reached for her diary to scribble down her thoughts. She wanted to write every detail about Texas— all the way from the Red River to her new home in Springfield. She wrote for a long, long time, telling exactly how she felt. How wonderful to live in the big state of Texas!

May 15, 1851

Dear Diary,

After over two months on the trail, we are finally in our new home. Texas is so big, and the countryside can be so different. After we left the Red River, we traveled through the piney woods of east Texas. The trees seemed to reach all the way to the sky and the ground was carpeted in pine needles. And we saw the most amazing trees I have ever seen! They were called dogwoods, and they were covered with beautiful white flowers. Once, we came upon some lovely red roses and I picked some for Mama. They smelled so wonderful. And the azaleas were breathtaking—whites, pinks, and magentas—and so fragrant. The further west we traveled, we left the piney woods and the landscape opened up into rolling hills, prairies, and grassland. The fields were covered with Texas bluebonnets. I could hardly tell where the flowers ended and the sky began. They are truly my favorite spring flower.

As our wagon rolled through the Indian grass, we saw many jackrabbits. They were the funniest-looking rabbits I have ever seen. They were large rabbits with long, long ears. Why, their ears were as long as their hind legs! One night, as we set up camp along a rocky bluff, we came upon a ringtail cat resting in the hollow of a tree. It didn't look like a cat at all but more like a raccoon. It had the face of a fox with large black eyes circled in white and a long, black-and-white ringed tail. The twins wanted to catch it and keep it, but Mama would have none of that.

We are finally in our new home in Springfield. It has beautiful trees and a stream, and there is a lake not too far away. I can't wait to go swimming in it. The fields are beautiful, and Papa wants to plant corn and wheat. I watched the sunset last night and thought it was the most beautiful sunset I had ever seen.

Thank You, God, for bringing us safely to our new home in Texas. And thank You for showing me how to trust in You.

Sincerely,
Katie Sue

She loved all of their new friends and neighbors and began to think of herself as a true "Texan."

HAPPY TO BE IN TEXAS!

KATIE SUE AND HER FAMILY SETTLED into their new life in Texas in no time at all. One morning, she awoke and looked out the back flap of the wagon. The sun was peeking through the clouds and casting its early morning reddish Texas glow onto the Herod farm. Just a few seconds later, its rays quickly dropped onto nearby Pole Cat Creek.

"What a beautiful sight!" she said to herself.

It didn't take long to get to know the other settlers in Springfield. They met the Turner family from Missouri. Katie Sue smiled as she saw their three youngsters—all under the age of five. Mrs. Turner had her hands full, to be sure! Then they met the Warwick family from Arkansas. Mr. and Mrs. Warwick were an older couple with no children. Next, they met the Summers family from Virginia. Eight children! Eight. And seven of them were rambunctious boys who made the twins giggle with glee. After that, they met the Winslow family from North Carolina. The Winslow's had six children, and four of them were girls. Thank goodness! Why, Katie Sue had three new friends right away.

Their closest neighbors were the Powell family. A young man named Joseph looked to be about nineteen or twenty, and his two brothers a bit older. They'd floated all the way down the mighty Mississippi on their journey to Texas. Joseph, who went by the name of "Hitch" would be the schoolteacher. He and Papa seemed to hit it off right away. There were several other families nearby, and all of them seemed quite nice, also.

"See! You fretted for nothing," Papa said with a grin, tugging on her braid. "I told you there would be lots of new friends in Texas."

"You were right!" She gave her father a hug and thanked him for bringing the family to their new home.

They even met some of the "old-timers" who had settled in the area around 1838. They told Katie Sue and her family the story about the Parker family who came to Texas in 1833 and built Fort Parker for protection from the Indians. But on May 19, 1836, that protection tragically failed them. The Comanche and other neighboring Indian tribes attacked the fort, killing many of the Parker family and taking five prisoners. Four of the prisoners were eventually released, but one girl named Cynthia Ann Parker, who was nine at the time of the raid, was not among the freed prisoners. It was said that she had become one of the Comanche and had even married a Comanche chief!

Katie Sue thought the story was both shocking and mysterious. What if they were attacked by Indians and taken prisoner? Why the very thought of it sent chills up and down her spine. She decided this was yet another area where she would have to trust God and pray for His protection for her and her family.

Within days of settling in, Papa started building their new house. Several of the menfolk came to help him. Katie Sue watched in amazement as the trees were cut down and the logs were chinked together. How amazing, to think that a tree could become a house! And to watch the men work in the heat of summer—how could they stand it? She and the other children played in the creek to keep cool.

Months later, just as fall set in, they all stood and stared at the beautiful two-story home in awe.

"I can't believe it's done!" Mama said. "Finally! Our new home!"

Papa and the other men made new beds for the family then moved all the furniture into the house. For the first time in months, Katie Sue slept in a bed—a real, honest-to-goodness bed. The mattress was filled with feathers and was so soft, she could hardly believe it. After sleeping in the wagon for so long, she had almost forgotten what a real bed felt like!

As the Herods settled into their new home, Katie Sue began to feel like she was really part of a community again. She loved all of their new friends and neighbors and began to think of herself as a true "Texan." As the heat of the summer began to fade, Katie Sue and her new friends spent their time playing in the nearby lake. Katie Sue never knew that fishing and splashing in the water could be so much fun.

Late one afternoon as Katie Sue was coming back from a swim, she saw an alarming sight. Indians! Dozens of them surrounding their land and house! Where were Mama and Papa and her sisters? Terror gripped her heart while she stood paralyzed in fear. As she hid among the trees, she could hear her heart beating loudly in her ears. Or was that the sound of a drum? Katie Sue remembered the tragic story of the Parker family. Had God brought them here to Texas only to suffer the same fate? Immediately she reined in her wild thoughts and began to pray. She cried out to God for protection for her and her family. Tears streamed down her face as she fell to her knees and pleaded with God for her family to be safe.

Suddenly she heard a familiar sound. It was her sisters' laughing as in play. Katie Sue raised her tear-streaked face and through the blur of tears, she saw her sisters, running and playing with two small Indian children. She looked again and saw her mama and papa coming from behind the house with two Indian men following behind with a large deer, hung between two wooden poles. Katie Sue could hardly believe her eyes. Her family was safe after all. God had protected them. These Indians meant no harm, but instead, they were welcoming them! Katie Sue rushed over to her parents and fell into her father's arms.

"Oh Papa, you're safe! God kept you safe! I was so scared you were all hurt." Katie Sue cried in his arms until her tears dried up and she began to laugh.

"Katie Sue, of course we are safe. God's hand of protection is always upon us. We have only to trust in Him for all things."

Katie Sue smiled up into her father's face and thought about how safe she felt in his arms. It was just like being in the arms of her heavenly Father. She knew then that she could trust her papa, and she knew she could trust God.

As the fall began to take over summer, Papa and the other men met together to discuss building the new school which would also be used for church services on Sunday.

"We've been needing a church around here," Mr. Turner said. "Lots of folks haven't worshipped together in a real church since they arrived."

"I figured as much," Papa said, "and more will be arriving before you know it. There will be dozens of families in Springfield by the fall, I feel sure. Dozens."

"And more by next spring," Mr. Turner added, "so building a schoolhouse that doubles as a church makes a lot of sense. And of course we will need someone to preach. How do you feel about that, James?"

Katie Sue's Papa smiled broadly. "I do believe the Lord has called me to preach," he said. "So I would be more than happy to fill the pulpit. That is why God called me to Texas, to build churches and share God's love with those who don't know Him."

And so it was agreed. The folks of Springfield built the church by the early fall and had their first-ever service together. Fourteen families met together that day to worship God. Mama led in song, her beautiful voice filling the room. As the others joined in, Katie Sue couldn't help but think they sounded like a heavenly choir. She thought back to their church in Tennessee, and all of their friends there. She missed them, of course, but wouldn't trade her new church for the old one. There was something quite special about being part of this new church family that just felt right.

Papa stood to preach, his eyes bright with joy. With a smile on his face, he read a familiar scripture from his big black Bible in Proverbs 3:5-6. "*Trust in the LORD with all thine heart; and lean not unto thine own under-*

standing. In all thy ways acknowledge him, and he shall direct thy paths."

As Papa began to preach, Katie Sue thought about those words one more time. She had trusted in the Lord with her whole heart—trusted Him to see her through the journey from Tennessee to Texas, trusted Him to fill the aching spot in her heart after leaving her best friend, Matilda, behind, and trusted Him to begin a new life in a new place.

"God is trustworthy," Papa said from the front of the room. "We can count on Him to help us when we can't help ourselves. He will make our paths straight, even when we aren't sure which way to go."

After the church service came to a close, all of the families met together for a picnic on the lawn. Katie Sue wasn't sure when she'd ever seen such wonderful foods! Her tummy was quite full within no time. Afterwards, she and her new friends ran and played together. What fun they had! Every now and again she would look at her locket and think of Matilda. She would imagine her friend right there alongside her—in Texas.

"I know what I will do!" Katie Sue grinned as an idea came to her. "I will send my diary to Matilda. She will love reading about my travels!" The more she thought about it, the more excited she grew. Her best friend would have a wonderful time reading about how she had crossed the

Mississippi on a ferry and how she had played with the Caddo Indian children at the Red River.

And wouldn't Matilda be surprised at what a tomboy she'd become! Why Katie Sue loved playing outside now just as much as the twins did.

Just as the others finished up their playtime and their mothers began to pack up the foods, Katie Sue slipped into the church. She sat in the back pew and looked around at the tiny building, amazed at all God had done.

She bowed her head and began to pray. She thanked God for all of the people He had brought into her life, and she thanked Him for bringing her family safely from Tennessee to Texas. She thanked Him for her new home, the church and school, and all the new friends she had already made.

Most of all, she thanked Him for the changes that had taken place in her own heart. She truly felt like a different person than the one she'd left behind in Tennessee. Here in Texas, she was stronger and braver, to be sure.

Katie Sue smiled as she thought about it. She felt like a…what was the word Papa always used? Oh yes! She felt like a pioneer! Gone was the girl who was scared of adventure. Here to stay was Katie Sue, the pioneer.

Grand Doll offered up a beautiful prayer, asking the Lord to watch over Chelsea Marie as she moved to Indiana and to give her new friends and a wonderful new school to attend.

Trusting God in All Things

C HELSEA MARIE LOOKED UP AT HER grandmother with a broad smile as the story came to a close. "Oh, Grand Doll, thank you for telling me about Katie Sue!"

"I thought you might like her story," Grand Doll said. "In many ways, she reminds me of you. She had to leave her home and her friends behind to travel to a new place."

"And she was in our family?" Chelsea Marie asked. "Really?"

"Oh yes!" Grand Doll said. "After all, how do you think our family came to live in Texas?"

"I guess I never thought about it," Chelsea Marie said with a shrug.

"Katie Sue and her family settled right here in this area. In fact, the park you are in today, Fort Parker, is next to where the old town of Springfield is located. You might be walking on the very same ground where Katie Sue played."

"Wow!" Chelsea Marie exclaimed.

"The Herods traveled all the way from Tennessee to Texas. They were true pioneers."

Chelsea Marie looked down at the ground and shrugged. "If I move to Indiana, will that make me a pioneer too?"

Grand Doll chuckled. "I suppose you could call it that. Pioneers were adventurous people. People who trusted God. People who liked to try new things. I dare say, you have an adventurous spirit and you are very brave!"

A deep sigh rose up from inside Chelsea Marie. "I want to be like that," she said finally. "Even if it's hard, I want to trust God."

"I know you do, honey," Grand Doll said. "That's why I told you the story. I knew if you heard it, you would be reminded that God is trustworthy. No matter what you're going through, He is right there, going through it with you. And…," a twinkle lit her eyes as she spoke, "I have the locket at my house."

"W…what?" Chelsea Marie looked up, amazed. "You have Katie Sue's locket?"

"I sure do!" Grand Doll said, "Of course, the photos inside have been replaced many times. I have a picture of myself in it when I was a little girl. If you will remind me next time you are at my house, I will show you the locket."

"Oh, Grand Doll! That would be wonderful."

"There is more to the story, if you would like to hear it," Grand Doll said with a wink.

"Really?" Chelsea Marie bounced up and down in excitement. "Tell me, please!"

Her grandmother chuckled. "Katie Sue grew up and got married on Christmas Day in that same little church where her papa preached. She married Hitch Powell. Do you remember who he was?"

"The schoolteacher?"

"That's right. Katie Sue's papa, James Herod, along with Hitch Powell, started several churches and schools around the state. In fact, the school Katie Sue attended was the very first school in all of central Texas."

"Wow!" Chelsea Marie said. "That's so cool."

"And not only did James Herod preach and farm, but he was a medical doctor as well. He attended to both the spiritual and physical needs of the people."

"So you see, honey," Grand Doll continued, "even though Katie Sue's father gave up a lot—sold his cotton gin and his blacksmithing business back in Tennessee— God gave him the desires of his heart in a new place. He will do the same for you. I know He will."

"Really?"

"Really." Her grandmother gave her hand a squeeze. "Now, would you mind if I prayed with you before we head back to the campsite to meet the others?"

"Please!" Chelsea Marie said. "That would make me feel so much better." She loved it when her grandmother prayed.

Grand Doll offered up a beautiful prayer, asking the Lord to watch over Chelsea Marie as she moved to Indiana, and to give her new friends and a wonderful new school to attend. After the prayer, Chelsea Marie felt better.

"Now, are you ready to join the others for hot dogs and homemade ice cream?" Grand Doll asked.

"Oh, yes ma'am!" Chelsea Marie answered.

They headed back down the trail toward the campsite, hand in hand. Before long, Grand Doll began to sing in a pure, sweet voice: *"Trust and obey, for there's no other way to be happy in Jesus, than to trust and obey."*

Chelsea Marie listened quietly then began to hum along. Soon, she was singing along at the top of her lungs. *"Trust and obey, for there's no other way to be happy in Jesus, than to trust and obey."*

She smiled as she thought about all of the things she had learned from Katie Sue's remarkable story. She could be adventurous! She could be a pioneer! And she could certainly trust God through all of the changes in her life—the little ones and the big ones.

With Grand Doll's hand tightly clutched in her own, she skipped back to the campsite to enjoy the rest of the evening with those she loved.

Fun Facts
and More

§ In the 1800s, thousands of American pioneers moved by wagon train from the East Coast to unsettled territories in the West.

§ Many families sold their possessions to get the necessary money to travel across the country by wagon to their new homes.

§ The wagons that pioneers traveled in were usually made of hickory, oak, or maple wood.

§ Wagon trains traveled in caravans and gathered in a circle at night when they camped out. Evenings on the trail were often spent singing, playing the fiddle, telling stories, and reading from the Bible.

§ At least one schoolteacher usually traveled along with the caravan to teach the children their lessons.

§ Most westward bound wagon trains traveled between fifteen and twenty miles per day. On rainy days, they traveled much slower.

§ Bad weather along the trail was reason for concern. Not only could a storm slow down a wagon train, lightning from the storms often caused fires.

§ Children kept busy with chores on the trail. They milked cows, fetched water, and helped care for younger brothers and sisters.

§ Texas is the only state that was ever a country (republic) first! Because of that, Texas is the only state that can fly its flag as high as the American flag.

§ There has always been a great kinship between the people of Tennessee and the people of Texas. Several brave men from Tennessee fought alongside Texans at the famous Battle of the Alamo.

Questions to Ponder

§ What does it mean to trust God? Is God trustworthy?

§ Can you relate to Katie Sue's struggle? Have you ever had to trust God through changes in your own life?

§ What is the hardest thing about moving from one place to another?

§ Is making new friends an easy thing to do?

§ What would be the hardest thing about traveling by wagon train? What would be the best thing?

§ If you could choose between living in Tennessee and living in Texas, which one would you choose?

§ How do the chores the children performed on the trail compare to your chores?

§ Have you ever been on a campout? If so, what was it like?

§ Wagon trains usually traveled about fifteen miles per day. How many miles per day does your family travel when you're on the road?

§ Katie Sue learned not to judge people by their outward appearance. Can you think of a time when you judged someone unfairly?

What Is Trust?

EBSTER'S DICTIONARY DEFINES TRUST as "assured reliance on the character, ability, strength, or truth of someone or something...dependence on something...hope." [1]

The Bible's definition takes it further and defines trust as being totally dependent on God. It means "belief, reliance, support, and confidence in the Lord." Trust is a decision. It is resting in God and being totally confident in the Lord to do what He has promised.

Some simple definitions for trust are:

§   Not trying to always "do it yourself"
§   Believing that God can do what He promises
§   Depending on the Lord to act on your behalf

Trust is depending on someone bigger than you. Have you ever tried to do something and not asked for

---

[1]*Merriam Webster's Collegiate Dictionary, 11th Edition*, s.v. "Trust."

help and found out you couldn't do it? Then, when you finally asked for help from someone you trusted (your parents, sisters or brothers, a friend, or God), did it make a difference?

_____

_____

To trust is to believe in someone who knows what is best for you. Trust is having confidence that your parents know what you need, when you need it. Just like God, godly parents are watching over you and supplying your needs. Give an example of how you have trusted in your parents and how they have met your need:

_____

_____

Let's look at people in the Bible who have exhibited trust in God:

RUTH: RUTH 2:11-12 NKJV

And Boaz answered and said to her, "It has been fully reported to me, all that you have done for your mother-in-law since the death of your husband, and how you have left your father and your mother and the land of your birth, and have come to a people whom you did not know before. The LORD repay your work, and a full reward be given you by the LORD God of Israel, under whose wings you have come for refuge."

The story of Ruth is an amazing story. She left her family, country, and everything she had ever known to follow her mother-in-law and to follow God. But in the end, she was blessed. Read the story of Ruth in your Bible. Write down everything she left behind (good and bad) and then write down all the ways she was blessed in the end.

_____

_____

_____

_____

What example does Ruth give us about trust?

_____

_____

_____

_____

Give an example of how this applies to your life? What have you had to "give up" in order to do what the Lord has asked you to do?

_____

_____

_____

_____

DANIEL AND KING DARIUS:
DANIEL 6:16,18-23 NKJV

So the king gave the command, and they brought Daniel and cast him into the den of lions. But the king spoke, saying to Daniel, "Your God, whom you serve continually, He will deliver you." ... Now the king went to his palace and spent the night fasting; ... Then the king arose very early in the morning and went in haste to the den of lions. ... The king spoke, saying to Daniel, "Daniel, servant of the living God, has your God, whom you serve continually, been able to deliver you from the lions?" Then Daniel said to the king, "O king, live forever! My God sent His angel and shut the lions' mouths, so that they have not hurt me, because I was found innocent before Him; and also, O king, I have done no wrong before you." … So Daniel was taken up out of the den, and no injury whatever was found on him, because he believed in his God.

Not only did Daniel have to trust in God, but King Darius did as well. They both trusted that God would deliver Daniel, because Daniel was innocent. Our trust will not usually get us thrown into lions' dens, but sometimes it might cause us to be in uncomfortable situations. Has trusting in God ever put you in a situation that was less than comfortable?

_____

_____

_____

Sometimes we have to trust our parents, even when we are scared. Write about a time when you had to trust in your parents and they kept you safe:

_____

_____

_____

MARY: LUKE 1:38 NKJV

Then Mary said, "Behold the maidservant of the Lord! Let it be to me according to your word." And the angel departed from her.

We have all heard the Christmas story and know that Mary is the mother of Jesus, the Son of God. That alone makes her special. But Mary had to make a decision to trust God and believe His Word. Her decision not only impacted her and her family, but it impacted the entire world.

How did Mary show her trust in the Lord? What was required of her? How big did her trust in God need to be?

_____

_____

_____

_____

Mary was unique and no one else will have to do what she was called on to do. But, we each have the opportunity to show how much we depend on and trust the Lord.

What is one *big* thing you have been asked to do by God that almost seemed impossible, but you trusted in Him anyway?

_____

_____

_____

Now that you have a better understanding of trust, think of how the characters in this book were faced with the decision to trust. Give at least three examples of the way they showed their trust.

First example:

_____

_____

_____

_____

Second example:

_____

_____

_____

_____

Third example:

_____

_____

_____

_____

Give at least three examples in your own life of how you can use trust:

_____

_____

_____

Name at least three people that you believe you can trust with your life:

_____

_____

_____

_____

QUOTES FROM GODLY INDIVIDUALS THAT EXPRESS TRUST

Francis Scott Key, the author of "The Star Spangled Banner" had a deep faith and trust in God. He said this concerning our country: "And this be our motto, 'In God is our trust.'"[2]

Corrie ten Boom, author of *The Hiding Place*, has an amazing story to tell. She said this of trust: "When a train goes through a tunnel and it gets dark, you don't throw away the ticket and jump off. You sit still and trust the engineer."[3] In the same way, we must trust God when we are going through times of darkness.

Trust is learned and exercised by faith in Christ Jesus.

---

[2]Leonard Roy Frank, comp., *Quotationary* (New York: Random House, 2001, 1999), 879.

[3]Vern McLellan, comp., *Wise Words and Quotes* (Wheaton, Illinois: Tyndale House Publishers, 1998), 274.

Backyard Camping

OU DON'T HAVE TO BE IN THE WOODS TO have a campout. Backyard camping can be just as much fun. Get Mom and Dad to help organize a backyard campout for some weekend fun.

The first thing you should do is pitch a tent. If you already have one, pull it out of the garage and set it up. If you don't have one, get some large blankets and sheets and make your own tent. The easiest way to do this is to find something large to drape it over. You could use a picnic table or maybe some sawhorses. It doesn't have to be super big, just large enough to put a few sleeping bags under. And that is the next step after your tent is made. Grab your sleeping bags and set them up for the night. Don't forget your pillow.

One item you will always need while you're camping is a flashlight. Keep it with you so you know where it is when you need it.

The next thing you want to think about while camping out is a campfire. Since you can't have a real campfire in your backyard, ask your mom or dad if they can make a charcoal fire in the grill. Remember, kids, never play around a fire or grill. Make sure your parents are present whenever you are near it.

One of the fun things about camping out is the games you can play. There are so many outdoor games that are even more fun when you are camping out. Invite some friends or neighbors over to join you. Sometimes, more friends can mean more fun.

A campout and playing outside games can sure make you hungry. There are many dinners that are fun to prepare and eat outside. The easiest and most fun is to roast hot dogs over the charcoal grill. If you do not have grill sticks, you can use a wire coat hanger that has been straightened or even a long stick. Place your hot dog on the end of the stick and rotate it about every minute for even cooking. There is also another fun outdoor dinner and that is called a hobo dinner. In the food section, we will give you ideas on how to cook an awesome meal. Don't forget dessert. S'mores are always a hit when you are camping or cooking out. Roast your marshmallows on the same grill sticks you used for the hot dogs. Have your graham crackers and chocolate bars ready. When your marshmallows are done, sandwich them between the graham crackers and chocolate. They are melt-in-your-mouth delicious.

After a fun day of setting up camp, playing games, and preparing and eating dinner, you will be ready to wind down and relax. No campout is complete without singing some camp songs. Gather everyone around in a circle and join in for some singing fun. After the singing is finished, you might want to offer up a prayer of thanks for the wonderful day you have had. Be sure to look at all the beautiful stars in the sky. Spending time outdoors is a good time to admire God's handiwork and be thankful for everything He has made. With a prayer on your lips, and a flashlight in your hand, make your way to your tent and climb in your sleeping bag. But don't go to sleep just yet. Using your flashlight, you can make shadows on the tent wall with your hands.

Camping out can be tons of fun for you and your family and friends.

Outdoor Games

*T*HERE ARE MANY OUTDOOR GAMES YOU can play that are fun for you, your family, and friends. Here are just a few suggestions. If you don't know how to play them, ask your parents or grandparents and maybe even do some research to find out how they are played.

§ Hide-and-seek
§ Tag
§ Swinging Statues
§ Freeze Tag
§ Red Rover
§ Red Light, Green Light
§ Duck, Duck, Goose
§ Potato Sack Races
§ Three-legged Race
§ Egg Toss

ERE ARE A FEW DO-IT-YOURSELF recipes that are sure to be a hit at any campout or cookout!

HOT DOGS & HAMBURGERS

§ Hot dogs

§ Hot dog buns

§ Hamburger patties

§ Hamburger buns

§ All the fixings (ketchup, mustard, lettuce, tomato, pickles)

Nothing can beat the great American hot dog. When you are able to roast it over an open fire or charcoal grill, the taste is second to none. In the case you can't, a hot dog on the propane grill can be just as good. If you are firing up the grill, you can even add hamburgers to the dinner menu. Hot dogs and hamburgers are a great combination for your cookout.

HOBO DINNERS

A hobo dinner is fun and easy to prepare. Here is what you need per person:

- § 1 hamburger patty (uncooked)
- § 1 medium potato (sliced or diced with skins on or off)
- § 6 – 10 baby carrots
- § Salt and pepper or other seasoned salt
- § 1 tablespoon butter
- § 1 sheet of foil (about 12 – 15 inches long)

Place hamburger patty in the middle of the foil. Layer potatoes and carrots. Add seasoning and top with butter. Fold all four ends of foil together to form a seal. Place foil packets on a grill over the coals or on the propane grill or even in the oven at 350 degrees. Cook for about 30 minutes. Take off the grill and open up foil and check meat for doneness. If the meat is not fully cooked, place back on the grill for 5 to 10 minutes.

CAMPING CORN ON THE COB

- § Ears of fresh corn
- § Butter
- § Salt
- § Foil

Here is a great addition to any camping menu. Take ears of corn and wash. Place on sheet of foil and coat with butter and salt. Wrap up tightly in the foil. Place on grill (or in the oven) and cook about 30 minutes.

BISCUIT ON A STICK

- § 1 can biscuits
- § Butter
- § Jelly or honey, if desired

This is a fun way to make biscuits. They are a good addition to your hobo dinner. Take each individual biscuit and flatten out to about ½" thickness. Wrap around the end of your skewer, making sure it is secure. Cook over charcoal or propane grill until biscuit has risen and turned golden brown. Remove from heat and skewer and add butter in the middle. Add jelly or honey, if desired.

S'MORES

§ Marshmallows

§ Chocolate bars

§ Graham crackers

Nothing says camping out like making homemade s'mores. Skewer the marshmallows and place over charcoal or propane grill. Rotate often for even cooking. When marshmallow is golden brown, sandwich in between two graham crackers and a piece of chocolate.

BAKED APPLES

§ Apple of your choice

§ Butter

§ Cinnamon

Here is a dessert that is easy and fun to make. Take your favorite apple and core it without separating the apple. Add butter and plenty of cinnamon inside the apple. Wrap in foil. Place in the coals of the charcoal grill or in the oven for 30 to 45 minutes. Apple is done when the inside is soft.

EASY HOMEMADE ICE CREAM

Per person:

§ ½ cup milk

§ ¼ cup half-and-half

§ 1 Tbs. sugar

§ ¼ teaspoon vanilla

§ 1 sandwich size zip bag

§ 1 gallon size zip bag

§ 2 cups ice

§ 1 tablespoon rock salt

§ Favorite topping

In smaller zip bag, add the milk, half-and-half, sugar, and vanilla. Seal tightly. In the larger bag, add the ice, salt, and smaller zip bag, and seal tightly. Shake vigorously for about five to ten minutes. Remove zip bag containing ice cream and rinse or wipe with cold water to remove salt on outside of bag. Open carefully and dig in. You can top with your favorite topping.

*S*INGING WITH YOUR FRIENDS AND FAMILY is a fun way to spend the evening. Listed are some "old songs" that you should enjoy. If you don't know the tune, ask your parents or grandparents. Someone is sure to know. Happy singing!

CLEMENTINE

A song about a miner in the California gold rush of 1849.

In a cavern, in a canyon,
Excavating for a mine,
Dwelt a miner, forty-niner,
And his daughter, Clementine.

Oh, my darling, oh, my darling,
Oh, my darling, Clementine,
You are lost and gone forever,
Dreadful sorry, Clementine.

OH! SUSANNA

Katie Sue and her family sang this song on the trail.

Oh, I come from Alabama with a banjo on my knee,
And I'm goin' to Louisiana, my true love for to see.
It rained all night the day I left, the weather it was dry,
The sun so hot I froze to death, Susanna, don't you cry.

Oh, Susanna, oh, don't you cry for me.
For I come from Alabama, with my banjo on my knee.

I had a dream the other night when everything was still.
I thought I saw Susanna coming up the hill.
The buckwheat cake was in her mouth, a tear was in
*   her eye.*
I said I'm coming from Dixieland, Susanna don't you
*   cry.*

Oh, Susanna, oh, don't you cry for me.
For I come from Alabama, with my banjo on my knee.

THE OLD GRAY MARE

An old folk song sung for generations.

Oh, the old gray mare, she ain't what she used to be,
Ain't what she used to be, ain't what she used to be.
The old gray mare, she ain't what she used to be,
Many long years ago.
Many long years ago, many long years ago.
The old gray mare, she ain't what she used to be,
Many long years ago.

The old gray mare, she kicked on the whiffletree,
Kicked on the whiffletree, kicked on the whiffletree
The old gray mare, she kicked on the whiffletree
Many long years ago.
Many long years ago, many long years ago,
The old gray mare, she kicked on the whiffletree
Many long years ago.

ROW, ROW, ROW YOUR BOAT

This song is fun when it is sung in rounds. One group
starts, and then the other follows.

Row, row, row your boat,
Gently down the stream.
Merrily, merrily, merrily, merrily,
Life is but a dream.

MY BONNIE LIES OVER THE OCEAN

This is an old Scottish folk song.

My Bonnie lies over the ocean,
My Bonnie lies over the sea.
My Bonnie lies over the ocean,
Oh, bring back my Bonnie to me.

Bring back, bring back,
Oh, bring back my Bonnie to me, to me.
Bring back, bring back,
Oh, bring back my Bonnie to me.

Oh, blow ye the winds o'er the ocean,
And blow ye the winds o'er the sea.
Oh, blow ye the winds o'er the ocean,
And bring back my Bonnie to me.

Bring back, bring back,
Oh, bring back my Bonnie to me, to me.
Bring back, bring back,
Oh, bring back my Bonnie to me.

The winds have blown over the ocean.
The winds have blown over the sea.
The winds have blown over the ocean,
And brought back my Bonnie to me.

Bring back, bring back,
Oh, bring back my Bonnie to me, to me.
Bring back, bring back,
Oh, bring back my Bonnie to me.

The Eleanor Series

ELEANOR CLARK CONCEIVED THE IDEA for *The Eleanor Series* while researching her family's rich American history. Motivated by her family lineage, which had been traced back to the early 17th century, a God-ordained idea emerged: the legacy left by her ancestors provided the perfect tool to reach today's children with the timeless truths of patriotism, godly character, and miracles of faith. Through her own family's stories, she instills in children a love of God and country, along with a passion for history. With that in mind, she set out to craft this collection of novels for the youth of today. Each story in *The Eleanor Series* focuses on a particular character trait, and is laced with the pioneering spirit of one of Eleanor's true-to-life family members. These captivating stories span generations, are historically accurate, and highlight the nation's Christian heritage of faith. Twenty-first century readers—both children and parents—are sure to relate to these amazing character-building stories of young Americans while learning Christian values and American history.

LOOK FOR ALL OF THESE BOOKS IN THE ELEANOR SERIES:

Visit our Web site at: www.eleanorseries.com

About the Author

Eleanor Clark lives in central Texas with Lee, her husband of over 50 years, and as matriarch of the family, she is devoted to her 5 children, 17 grandchildren, and 5 great grandchildren.

Born the daughter of a Texas sharecropper and raised in the Great Depression, Eleanor was a female pioneer in crossing economic, gender, educational, and corporate barriers. An executive for one of America's most prestigious ministries, Eleanor later founded her own highly successful consulting firm. Her appreciation of her American and Christian heritage comes to life along with her exciting and colorful family history in the youth fiction series, *The Eleanor Series.*